D1598261

32: Portugal
in Revolution

THE WASHINGTON PAPERS
Volume III

32: Portugal
in Revolution

Michael Harsgor

THE CENTER FOR STRATEGIC AND INTERNATIONAL STUDIES
Georgetown University, Washington, D.C.

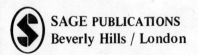

SAGE PUBLICATIONS
Beverly Hills / London

For information address:

SAGE PUBLICATIONS, INC.
275 South Beverly Drive
Beverly Hills, California 902 12

SAGE PUBLICATIONS LTD
St George's House / 44 Hatton Garden
London EC1N 8ER

International Standard Book Number 0-8039-0647-1

Library of Congress Catalog Card No. 76-2250

FIRST PRINTING

---

*When citing a Washington Paper, please use the proper form. Remember to cite
the series title and include the paper number. One of the two following formats
can be adapted (depending on the style manual used):*

(1) HASSNER, P. (1973) "Europe in the Age of Negotiation." The Washington
Papers, I, 8. Beverly Hills and London: Sage Pubns.

OR

(2) Hassner, Pierre. 1973. *Europe in the Age of Negotiation.* The Washington
Papers, vol. 1, no. 8. Beverly Hills and London: Sage Publications.

CONTENTS

I. INTRODUCTION

Portugal has long been considered an historical paradox. Together with France it ranks as the oldest of present-day Western European states. When Portugal was proclaimed a kingdom in 1140, the United Kingdom, Spain, Italy, and Germany did not yet exist as coherent political entities. The new kingdom was to become remarkable for its territorial stability, as well as other attributes. Indeed, Portugal possesses the world's most settled continental frontier, its boundaries having remained practically unchanged since the second half of the thirteenth century.

Since the waning of the Middle Ages, this small country (population 8,063,100)—91,530 sq. km. with the adjoining archipelagos of Madeira and Azores, 88,530 sq. km. without them—had been the center of a wide seaborne empire whose appearance and disappearance were to mark the beginning and the end of Western colonialism. Following the example of Manuel the Fortunate (1495-1521), the kings of Portugal called themselves "lords of the conquest, navigation and commerce of India, Ethiopia, Arabia and Persia." Since the sixteenth century, the sixfold synthesis of navigator, trader, conqueror, colonial administrator, civilizer, and missionary had expressed the highest aim of the Portuguese in history. It must be noted that not a single one of these activities had any application to continental Portugal. For its elite the neglected mother country was like a royal estate. Lisbon with its fashionable social life served firstly as a stepping-stone to an imperial career and finally as a luxurious place of retirement. For centuries local production was less important for the national economy than imported goods, and this in turn determined royal policy.

So the country went through cycles of dependence on sugar, precious woods, gold, coffee, and diamonds. Only in the last and present centuries could sardines and wolfram be added to the list of products of European Portugal. Quite possibly, the April 1974 coup interrupted this series on the eve of a new oil cycle and of a renewed diamond one, stemming from the riches of Angola.[1]

Certainly it interrupted an unbroken line of Portuguese political thought that had always seen in empire and trade the bulwark of national independence. And this was no empty theorizing. Annexed by Spain in 1580 under the cover of a personal union between the two crowns, reluctant Portugal waited for the first good occasion to break the foreign yoke. The union with Spain, more than it hurt national pride, brought a loss in foreign trade and disastrous taxation. The opportunity for freedom presented itself in 1640. An almost bloodless revolution—as Portuguese revolutions generally are, compared with Spanish ones—brought to the throne the house of Braganza, which was only overthrown in 1910.

If for Portugal the eighteenth century was uneventful and complacent, disturbed only by the tragic Lisbon earthquake of 1755 and the ruthless attempt of the marquess of Pombal to put Portuguese administration on the same level as that of the most developed countries of Western Europe, the nineteenth century presented itself as an era of civil disturbances and general decadence.[2] In an atmosphere of restlessness and discontent, endemic civil wars, punctuated by military coups, gave way to a quieter constitutional practice only in the middle of the second half of the century. But already republicanism was gaining ground. Both the monarchy and the republican opposition saw in the renewal of colonial greatness the supreme panacea for Portugal's ills. It was partly because of its alleged weakness in dealing with foreign colonial powers that the monarchical regime was overthrown in the October 1910 republican revolution.[3]

The Portuguese only realized the importance of their African possessions after losing Brazil, in the twenties of the last century. Important expeditions were carried on after 1832, eastwards from Angola and westwards from Mozambique. The effective occupation of both these colonies and of Guinea ceased to be limited to narrow strips of coastal territory. From the beginning Portuguese colonialism was, at least in theory, not racist. The Constitution of 1822 had defined the nation as "the union of all the Portuguese of both hemispheres," and this principle, hallowed through following generations, gave birth to the basic myths of twentieth century Portuguese colonial practice (Marques, 1973: Vol. II, 63, 119-130), which before the last hundred years had rather belonged to a peculiar historical category aptly labeled "uneconomic imperialism" (by Hammond, 1966).

The First Republic (1910-1926) set out to change this state of affairs by developing a profitable colonialism, supposedly based on British and French models. But it did more; its ruling middle-class lawyers and mildly radical intellectuals felt encouraged to tackle the structural problems of Portuguese society: improvement of wage-earners' living standards, legislation for social welfare, agrarian reform, and action against the appallingly high illiteracy rates. Such basic reforms meant not only increased taxation for the rich but that some would pay taxes for the first time. Inevitably, the capitalists, landowners, foreign investors, and higher ranking bureaucrats felt that their interests were threatened; the generals and colonels were disgusted by the idea of radical notions infiltrating the army; and the clergy of all ranks, from the cardinal-patriarch of Lisbon to the village curate, were horrified by a regime whose first acts were inspired by the most extreme anticlericalism. But these strata of Portuguese society had never shown warm feelings for the Republic; it was weakened beyond any hope of recovery by the disaffection of precisely those social groups by whom and for whom it had been established: the middle and lower classes of Lisbon and Oporto, organized labor, petty officers of the army and the navy, and liberal intellectual circles. These groups were embittered by the incapacity of republican governments to fight inflation, the permanent riots, the extreme-leftist extravagances, the cult of anarchism, and the application of "revolutionary violence," factors that also led to the disillusionment with democracy of the public at large. Nevertheless, when the Republic was overthrown there were already signs that the regime had weathered the storm. The 1926 coup was timed to break out before public opinion could feel that the currency had become more stable, the budget more balanced, and the public debt lower.[4]

On May 28, 1926, the right-wing military junta started its coup in the conservative regions of northern Portugal. Lisbon did not budge. Five days later the democratic Republic was dead, killed more by the lassitude of the republican masses than by the violence of a band of oath-breaking officers. But the May 28 coup did nothing to alleviate the ailments it pretended to cure. After two years of incompetent military rule the financial situation had again worsened, and its intricacies were above the understanding of the governing generals and colonels. General Carmona, who had ousted the actual leader of the 1926 coup, General Gomes da Costa, and had had himself elected president of the Republic, was at a loss. Following the advice of its financial counselors, the military government turned to a Coimbra professor of economics, Antonio de Oliveira Salazar (born 1889), who had already served for a few days as finance minister of the military junta in 1926 but had resigned when the generals showed no inclination to grant him a free hand. In April 1928, Salazar again became finance minister, this time after having received the right to control all the financial activities and budgets of the various government services.

For nearly half a century the name of this statesman and that of the country he led were identified one with another. Few historical figures have so successfully misled subsequent writers and researchers about their lack of ambition and seemingly reluctant acceptance of office. Antonio de Oliveira Salazar was born at Vimieiro, a tiny village of the Beira Alta province. As an estate manager, his father belonged to a higher social stratum than Salazar's official biographers have admitted: the family owned at least three houses. Privately educated, with no experience of school friendships, Salazar was always uneasy in company. Strongly attached to his mother, he never married, later attributing his bachelorhood to patriotism.

Salazar soon perceived that the religious career his family wished him to follow no longer held the promise it had offered in earlier times. In 1921, even before starting an academic *cursus honorum* in economics (a field very few

Portuguese plowed in those days; Salazar was a founding member of an "Academic Center of Christian Democracy") he put forward his candidature and was elected a member of parliament. After a few days, realizing that nobody was yet interested in him, that the label "democracy" frightened those from whom he expected help, Salazar resigned his seat. He never concealed his contempt for a parliamentary system in which the country's elite was not recognized and given a free hand.

Back at Coimbra University Salazar tried hard to publicize his views in order to attract the kind of people whose backing he desired. In the same year, 1921, at a convention of commercial and industrial associations, he developed a theory of cheap public management by cutting social services and published a series of articles on this theme. In 1924 he was the outstanding figure at the Eucharistic Convention at Braga, "the Portuguese Rome." One year later, as the author of "O Bolchevismo e a Sociedade" (Bolshevism and Society), Salazar had already become the undisputed spiritual leader of the Portuguese right.

Once in the government as minister of finance, Salazar took the measure of his military colleagues. They seemed to him uncertain and divided, and so this coolly ambitious man was able to seize the reins of political power. Working with a small group of devoted followers who saw the ex-Coimbra professor as a local representative of a European fascist tendency, Salazar advanced toward the establishment of his own brand of dictatorship.[5] Prohibiting the activity of all political parties, cleverly dividing the ranks of the monarchists (who expected Salazar to be for the exiled king Manuel II what the English general Monk had been for the exiled Charles II), and banning the extreme fascist wing—the Blue Shirts, the taciturn and unassuming dictator imposed his own constitution in 1933. Portugal was turned into an *Estado Novo* (new state), a subdued Lusitanian, catholic version of a fascist regime. Actually the constitution only ratified the existing order of things. There was a National Assembly which for many years had been a stage for self-congratulatory speeches delivered by Salazarist agents and clients, and a Cooperative Chamber "uniting all classes" was established after the Italian Fascist model. The liberty of the press was suppressed, strikes were outlawed, and university professors with liberal leanings—some of them with world-wide reputations—were dismissed. Newspaper, book, and film censorship was introduced, which shocked the Western democracies by "its hysteria and absurdity" (Trend, 1957: 188). And above all, there was the all-pervading, ubiquitous secret political police, the PIDE, of which more later.

Salazarist Portugal survived a string of military and political revolts, and was powerfully encouraged by the issue of the Spanish Civil War (1936-1939). During World War II, Portugal imitated Spain by refusing to link its fate with Rome and Berlin, which did not, however, prevent Salazar from proclaiming a day of national mourning after Hitler's suicide. But the allied victory did force Salazar to announce a drastic liberalization of his Estado Novo. Shortly afterwards, however, a vast purge aimed at those who had shown signs of opposition, the dismissal of hundreds of civil servants and army officials, and a tightening of the repressive machinery only proved that Salazarism was incapable of democratizing itself (Payne, 1973: 671).

In a changing world the Portuguese dictatorship stood out in its grim and eerie immobility. Backward, cowed into submission, a European country was ruled by senile generals and admirals, by a swarm of spies, and by a band of faceless bureaucrats all under the rod of a terrible old man. The social landscape seemed unalterable. Religion and official ideology were presented as immutable factors with obedience the highest virtue. Private property being the supreme value, a man was as good as his goods. Political power having been granted from above to Doctor Salazar, one had to humble oneself before the priest, bow to the policeman, and keep a respectful silence for fear of the PIDE agent. Salazar himself seemed eternal. When he fell from his chair in 1968, disabled till his death, a prostrated nation could not believe it.

II. THE STAGE IS SET

At the end of Salazar's reign, in September 1968, the Portuguese colonial empire was still enormous; in fact after the dismantling of the British and French colonial empires, it was the greatest concentration of territories under the control of a European state. It was formed by three main lumps, all of them in Africa, and by a string of small former "maritime stations," left over from the old Lusitanian mastery of the seas (see Wheeler and Pelissier, 1971; Davidson, 1973; and Newitt, 1973).

Angola, with its 1,246,700 sq. km., was the brightest jewel in the colonial crown. According to a 1960 census, it had a population of 4,832,677 inhabitants (density per sq. km.: 3.9); and was followed, in order of importance, by Mozambique, with 784,961 sq. km. and 6,592,994 inhabitants (density: 8.4); and by Guinea-Bissau, 36,125 sq. km. and 544,184 inhabitants (density 15.1). Along the western coast of Africa, Portugal possessed the Cabo Verde islands, (3,984 sq. km., 205,000 inhabitants, density 50.6), the "province of São Tomé and Príncipe," consisting of two islands, and until 1961 the dependency of São João Batista da Ajuda (964 sq. km., 63,676 inhabitants, density 66.1), an enclave within Dahomey. In the Indonesian archipelago, Portugal's flag flew above half of the Timor island (14,925 sq. km., 517,079 inhabitants, density 34.6); and in Asia, after the loss of the "Estado da Índia" (Portuguese India) conquered by Indian forces in December 1961, Portugal was left with the Chinese city of Macao (15.52 sq. km., 169,299 inhabitants, density ca. 112).

In peaceful times an army of 10,000 men was quite sufficient to defend this vast empire. The Lisbon government had tried to increase considerably the number of white-Portuguese colonists at least in the two big African territories. Yet by the middle of the present century the proportions of native versus white population groups were still 97.4 percent to 1.9 percent in Angola, 98.5 percent to 0.8 percent in Mozambique, and 98.7 percent to 0.8 percent Mestizos in

Guinea-Bissau. The attempt to direct emigrants from their Brazilian or European goals toward Africa ended in failure. In spite of the fact that the terms "colonies" and "empire" were officially dropped in favor of *Ultramar* (overseas territories), and that according to the Salazarist Foreign Minister Franco Nogueira, writing in 1967, the Portuguese considered themselves "to be an African nation,"[6] the actual African nations did not consider themselves to be Portuguese. Indeed, in the 76 years of this century, the Ultramar has not allowed its white rulers many days of peace and quiet. Military campaigns took place in Angola and Mozambique, and especially in Guinea, between 1913 and 1915. There were native uprisings in the 1920s, and police operations were needed to put down agitation in Guinea during the 1930s. It was enough to read the literature produced by the not very numerous black and mulatto young intellectuals to feel the growing African resentment of colonialism; yet it was precisely these "assimilated" natives on whom the Lisbon regime staked its greatest hopes of African-Lusitanian integration. But instead of "Lusitanism's heralds" in the dark continent, the cultural elites of the colonies quite naturally developed into a vanguard against Portuguese rule.[7]

The Angolan uprising started with hundreds of members of the *Movimento Popular de Libertação de Angola* (MPLA) attacking official buildings in Luanda in February 1961. Uprisings followed in Guinea (1963) and in Mozambique (1964). The ruling Salazarists decided not to pull out. Their decision was not only dictated by the wish to defend vested interests, but it was also strongly felt that the shock of losing an empire would be sufficient to kill the regime, too. However, it was the very desire to prevent such an outcome by all means, above all by military means, that in the process destroyed the Estado Novo. But in Lisbon nobody saw the writing on the wall. During most of the 1960s, the threat presented by the African rebellions could be successfully contained. However, the price paid by a very poor country (nearly a million of its citizens were forced to look for work in France, Germany, Luxembourg, and other countries) and by a regime unable to assure its working population even minimal European living standards, had to be very high, in fact too high.[8] The moment of truth came with the brain injury that incapacitated Salazar, whose abilities had already been impaired by senility.

According to the 1933 constitution, the president of the republic, 74-year-old rear-admiral Américo Tomás, had to designate the new prime minister. Tomás stood in the center of a clique of dyed-in-the-wool elderly naval officers, die-hard last-ditchers, who were convinced that Portugal was on the verge of victory in all three colonies. Tomás personally was the enthusiastic inspirer of the policy of going the whole hog, in spite of (or because of) the fact he had never seen action. During World War I he commanded a conservancy boat, and spent the whole of his remaining military career in the cartographic service of the Navy. Tomás had later served Salazar as minister of the Navy from 1944 to 1958, earning the reputation of a yes-man, able to assuage the whims of the growingly suspicious dictator. The day of reckoning came in 1958, when the then-serving president of the republic, Craveiro Lopes, got sick of merely being Salazar's puppet. The reluctant president was punished on the spot, being struck from the official National Union list of candidates and losing his chance of standing for reelection. The easy-to-handle Tomás was chosen instead. On the occasion of the usual charade staged before every Salazar-style election, the official candidate was confronted by the honest but naive lawyer, Arlindo Vicente, candidate of the left, and by a dare-devil Air Force general, Humberto Delgado. Salazar could get his protege elected only by fraudulent means: thousands of votes given to Delgado "went lost" mysteriously. Salazar rewarded his obedient president of the republic by having him reelected in 1965. He punished Delgado by having him murdered by the PIDE, and chastised Delgado's family attorney, Dr. Soares, the future socialist leader, by exile.

During Tomás' reign increasing corruption and the disintegration that Salazar-ism was undergoing gathered momentum. A wave of persecutions engulfed Delgado's partisans. The bishop of Porto, who had dared to criticize the regime in an open letter to Salazar, was exiled, and in 1959 a plot by left-wing Catholics was uncovered. In 1961 political exiles captured a Portuguese liner, a gesture that aroused public opinion around the world. In the same year the Minister of Defense, Botelho Moniz, tried to overthrow Salazar, and in January 1962 a force of united communists, socialists, Catholics, and liberals stormed the military base at Beja, in a vain attempt to start a generalized anti-Salazarist revolt.[9] President Tomás' job in finding a successor for the ailing prime minister was made more difficult by Salazar, who regularly dismissed any politician whose capacities could seem to make him an heir apparent. Santos Costa had been sacrificed in such a way (in 1958), and the able Ultramar minister, Adriano Moreira, who had been regarded as a possible successor to the aging Salazar, had to pay for his talent and energy. Among those driven away from the center of politics, Marcello Caetano had even played the role of a "left-Salazarist leader," awakening the hope of a possible future democratization of the regime under his aegis. Born in 1906, an enthusiastic fascist in his youth (after a doctrinaire royalist phase), Caetano's progress reads like a model Salazarist curriculum vitae. In 1936 as a member of the Imperial Colonial Council he drafted the adminis-trative code of the Estado Novo and led the national commissariat for youth charged with indoctrinating the young with the Salazarist interpretation of fascism. Later he became minister of the presidency (1955), a kind of assistant prime minister. It was too much for his rivals among the influential extreme right-wing Salazarists, who had the dictator sack Caetano at the first cabinet reshuffle (1958). In 1962, in his capacity as president of the Classical University of Lisbon, Caetano irritated his highly placed enemies even more by resigning in protest over police disregard for academic autonomy.

It may seem bizarre that the Salazarist old guard turned to such a man, offering him the power they had tried to deny him for the last ten years.

Actually it was a symptom of the general crisis into which the Estado Novo was sinking, a crisis underlined by the shortage of leadership. There was also anxiety about the forces the former leader, with internal opposition tendencies, could let loose against a president who was merely an orthodox nonentity.

When sounded about his willingness to assume the premiership, Caetano no longer believed in the possibility of Portugal winning her three African wars. In a confidential paper transmitted to Salazar himself, Caetano had stated that the only possible solution was federalization resulting in the establishment of "United Portuguese States," in which the metropolis and its main excolonies would cooperate on an equal footing (Caetano; 1974: 17 ff). Called in for consultations by President Tomás, Caetano proposed holding general elections "as honest as possible" in the following year—1969—in order to give the country the opportunity of expressing its actual feelings about the wars waged to keep the Ultramar subject to the Lisbon government. The president brushed the suggestion aside, pointing out that if the future prime minister took a stand favoring the granting of self-determination to the colonies, the Portuguese High Command could very easily establish a dictatorship committed to the pursuit of the war. This fact only discloses the elementary truth about the regime Caetano was invited to head: basically, the Estado Novo, whatever its trappings, was a police state, and it remained from its inception to its demise an army-backed and army-directed form of dictatorship. Thus the generals told Caetano that if he wanted the premiership he had better give up any ideas of federalization. To make this point crystal-clear to the incumbent prime minister, brigadier Bettencourt Rodrigues, army minister in Caetano's first cabinet, agreed to serve only after enquiring about his new boss' "degree of resolution" on defending the Ultramar. It is evident that the new prime minister took office pledged to a policy in which he no longer believed (Caetano, 1974: 17 ff). '

The six years of "caetanism" were to be an era of relative economic expansion—at least until the 1973 October war and the OPEC oil price rise. They were years of very cautious and superficial liberalization, but also years of deepening political crisis and of fatal disaffection among the young and most dynamic members of the officers' corps. In the October 1969 elections, the two opposition groups won about 12 percent of the votes cast; but with no representation allotted to electoral minorities, the "new" National Assembly stayed as it was, an exclusive club of one-party representatives.[10] But, hedged in by the Salazarist old guard and by the military oligarchy, unable to organize a proper ruling group around himself, Caetano toed the conservative line. Freedom of the press was withheld, and the corporate framework of a Mussolini-like institution continued in Portugal, 30 years after the Duce's fall. No political parties were permitted, no amnesty was granted, freedom of association was denied, and, above all, there was to be no change in the most vital of all subjects, foreign policy.[11]

Caetano rapidly found himself in difficulties, for example, in his relations with the *União Nacional*—the one area in which his position should have seemed less threatened. The União Nacional, the extreme right-wing government party, and the single legal political party in the country, never played the role of the fascist party in Italy or the Nazi party in Germany. It was neither the privileged and monopolistic force backing the supreme leader, nor the regular and obligatory channel for political advancement. The real props of Salazar's rule were the army leadership and the PIDE. By 1968, the União Nacional was nothing more than an umbrella organization bringing together "leading citizens" on the eve of the peculiar electoral consultations allowed by Salazarist constitutional practice.

Caetano tried to reinvigorate the government party by the introduction of "young blood"—men under 35 years of age—and intellectuals believing or wishing to be thought of as believing in the Estado Novo ideology. It proved to be an uphill task. Most of the youngish local leaders and members of the free professions flatly refused to have anything to do with the União Nacional. The prime minister's enticements were fearfully turned down, as if they had been attempts to enroll a person in an illegal body of conspirators. In 1969, Caetano, feeling that with the party as it was, there was nothing more to be done, tried to reorganize it under a more appealing name: thus the *Ação Nacional Popular* (National People's Action) was unhappily born. But when he tried to establish a list of members intended to man the ANP central committee a feeling of acute uneasiness again made itself felt. Nobody wanted to sit on the central organ of the government party. Only two to three persons assented to a proposal made by the prime minister himself! (Caetano, 1974: 47 ff).

Such reluctance can be explained by the feeling of general crisis from which the regime appeared unable to extricate itself. Probably, however, Caetano's efforts were bound to be futile given the Salazarist political framework, which was not adapted to the free display of public initiative. One need only consider what happened to a single small group of young economists and lawyers who honestly tried to bring about a degree of democratization of public life. This was the SEDES, a union of left-of-center (in relative Portuguese terms!) liberal "technocrats." In spite of his vaguely liberal oratory, Caetano and his aides were too much Salazar's disciples not to show extreme distrust of anything that was not their own creation. But in the context of what was called an "opening policy" they accepted, albeit half-heartedly, that a political group not affiliated with the government party could be allowed at the beginning of the 1970s. However, the day members of SEDES started criticizing Caetanist policies, they were seen as a deadly threat. When, to Caetano's rage, names appeared among SEDES adherents that had formerly been known to belong to the socialist electoral commission (CEUD) and even to the electoral commission backed by a "progressivist" hodgepodge behind which loomed the Portuguese Communist Party (PCP), SEDES itself was treated as a dangerous foe. Finally, in 1973 SEDES' main leaders disgustedly resigned their mandate from the National

Assembly. Clearly the regime would not permit any liberalization by constitutional means, thus setting the stage for violent action.

Now, however, the loyalty of the army was in question. In the past, official Portugal had had full confidence in its armed forces. Of course there were few armies with such a long record of rebellions and mutinies, a phenomenon which ought rather to have diminished that confidence; but a common feature of the numerous military mutinies had been their lack of political radicalism. In spite of the banners unfurled, these movements were more like a scramble for spoils and rewards than attempts at achieving structural changes in society. The military risings expressed the wish of a given segment of the officers' corps to have a greater say in public affairs.[12] The fact that the main parts of the armed forces were now fighting three separate African wars was not considered in Lisbon as an extraordinary phenomenon, fraught with danger. Beginning with the last 20 years of the nineteenth century, a period of service in Africa had been considered an obligatory stage in the career of every self-respecting officer. All the main military figures who had played a role in Portuguese politics during these last 100 years started by asserting themselves in Angola or Mozambique before thrusting their ambition upon continental Portugal: for example, Mousinho de Albuquerque, Paiva Couceiro, Norton de Matos. (For studies inspired by Mousinho de Albuquerque, see Trend, 1957: 185, 194, n. 20). Unhappily for the Lisbon regime the military mentality had changed beyond recognition precisely during the period of extreme conservative Salazarist rule.

By the middle of the present century, subtle changes started to make themselves felt in the recruitment of officers. The modest prosperity now enjoyed by a small part of Portuguese society meant that educated young men no longer wished or needed to join the army. At the same time, young men from the lower-middle class, from small towns, and even from rural areas, started to replace the young gentlemen in the military academies. For these new types of officers, a military career served personal and financial needs, rather than offering the prospect of social promotion. The structure of Portuguese society appeared so antiquated that in spite of a limited and regionalized economic prosperity, young men without proper family connections could never achieve interesting and well-paid jobs, which were usually taken by the scions of well-established bourgeois or Salazarist bureaucrats. A successful self-made career was possible only for someone ready to do political dirty work, for instance, spying on his friends or on university comrades on behalf of the PIDE.[13]

By the beginning of the 1970s, the officer corps of the professional army (*Quadro Permanente,* QP) was already split. This is clearly shown by an analysis of the social origin of officers, more or less at the *tenente-coronel* (lieutenant-colonel) level. Above that rank were superior officers from Lisbon and Oporto "polite society," sons of *latifundia* owners, descendants of "colonel dynasties";

below it was an array of men who had come up from far humbler strata of Portuguese society, and who, in some cases, before getting their introductory courses at the military academy had to be taught how to use a knife and fork. In such a way, paradoxically, a regime based on a strong sense of tradition and social stability itself manufactured a petty officer corps of robust plebeian origin, which in spite of recent military promotion did not forget opinions and beliefs current in the circles they came from, which was bitterly critical of the finé Lisbon gentlemen who for centuries had treated people not belonging to the power elite with the utmost contempt. The paradox did not end with the formation of an army in which junior officers felt alienated from their superiors and vice versa. In the later sixties as the war became more dangerous, sons of "good families" shirked active service. It was relatively easy for such young men, who knew the ropes, to find shelter in a military ministry in continental Portugal or at least in a nonfighting service. So the young low-born officers were left to bear the brunt of war alone. As the shortage in the professional ranks became yearly more acute, the Salazar government was obliged to turn to the students, mobilize them at officer level, and send them to Africa to fight the revolutionary movements there. This yearly batch of academy-educated junior officers was called *milicianos*. Boys without academic education, but with studies at high school level behind them, furnished the milicianos with noncommissioned officers. These milicianos did not belong to the *Quadro Parmanente,* and were made to feel it. The bitterness with which a growing number of milicianos officers contemplated their military role is better understood when the atmosphere at the universities from which they came is considered.

After a period of distrust, during which the Salazar government closed down a number of academic institutions (School of Arts in Oporto and School of Pharmacy at Coimbra, both in 1928; School of Commerce in Oporto, in 1933), the university system started to progress, especially after the middle of the century, benefiting from the atmosphere of relative expansion. More and more young people enrolled in the three metropolitan universities. There was nearly a six-fold increase in the number of students during Salazar's rule: 1926–6,000 students; 1940–9,000; 1950–14,000; 1960–20,000; 1968–35,000.[14] The authorities, fearing communist influence, strictly controlled student activities. Every form of criticism or opposition was labelled "communist," but it was to no avail. Dictatorship was hated by the intellectuals on the campus. From time to time student leaders were called to account by the police authorities or the most militant young people had it out with the police. These lecture-hall struggles steeled whole generations of student elites and prepared young, educated Portugal for a relentless fight against the ruling tyranny in conditions quite unknown to other Western European students with the exception of Spain. As the PIDE spies were everywhere, methods of organization had to be conspiratorial. In such an atmosphere communist cells thrived and prospered. As one graduate-school revolutionary of those days, Maria Antonia Fiadeiro, wrote in later reminiscences, it was healthier to mistake a decent student for a PIDE agent than to mistake a PIDE agent for a decent student (in Carvalhas et al., 1974). So from the start, academic political struggle was not free from a traditional characteristic of Portuguese civic life: sectarianism, a burning suspiciousness and fear of the outside world, and a narrow-minded attachment to a certain group or party. And this party's object of fanatical fervor had to be messianic and redemptive, with no hope of world salvation outside it.

Such were the students, or many of them, that the unending colonial wars forced the Salazarist oligarchy to mobilize at officer level. So fascist Portugal imported shiploads of Trojan horses into its creaking empire. All the Lisbon rulers could think up as a solution for their colonial problems was to swell the numbers of soldiers, to expand an enormous army well beyond the country's capacity to support it. In the last year of Caetano's government there were 170,000 men under arms, 135,000 of them in Africa. The air force numbered 16,000; the navy had 18,000 men. The National Republican Guard, the actual Praetorian guard of the regime, had 10,000 well-trained men—half-soldiers, half-policemen—and the Paramilitary Security Police numbered 15,000. Portugal was forced to spend a minimum per capita amount of 63.27 U.S. dollars on military expenditure, with a per capita income of just over 1,000 U.S. dollars. The military budget represented 7 percent of the GNP, more than that of the United States (Maxwell, 1975b). But this expansion of military bulk was not followed by an improvement in the supreme command. The Institute of High Military Studies *(Instituto de Altos Estudos Militares),* through which colonels had to pass before being promoted brigadiers, was a bitter disappointment to the civil government. As Caetano himself wrote sarcastically (1974: 167):

> every time it was necessary to promote a high-ranking officer and to have him posted to a responsible job . . . it was confirmed that A had not recovered from his illness, that B could not be considered clever, that C was unfit for that peculiar appointment, that D was the right man, but for private reasons he could not be posted far away . . . it was hell.

Such were the well-born colonels whom the young low-born captains and lieutenants hated and/or despised.

The General Staff *(Corpo do Estado Maior),* which was formed by officers who went through a special school, enjoyed an unenviable reputation. It was considered a "self-segregated corps," haughty but technically deficient, lost in a cloudy realm of abstract military theorizing incapable of being of service to commanders on combat duty. With the doubtful help of the above-mentioned institutions, the Superior Council for National Defense *(Conselho Superior de Defesa Nacional)* assumed the supreme direction of military operations. One of the main obstacles it permanently encountered was the rather lordly non-chalence with which high-ranking officers of upper-class origin and the military bureaucratic elite fulfilled their duties. The Caetanist defense minister, Professor

Silva Cunha, made a real sensation when he asked his subordinates to start working at nine o'clock in the morning—"a beastly hour to wake a man." It seems evident that militarily the Portuguese power elite had got itself caught in a hopeless contradiction. It was waging wars that could not be won, yet it granted the supreme military command to incompetents. It promoted officers from classes outside its own circles, who were contemptuous of the elite. Finally it reinforced these officers with radical-minded milicianos, bearing prophecies of doom for everything the regime represented.

In any case there were added reasons for the low morale in the armed forces. As the shortage in the professional ranks became even more acute, the government was forced to permit even milicianos officers to enter the military academy so as to enjoy a position of equality with the Quadro Permanente officers, who now felt their status endangered. However, the milicianos were also bitter, when they discovered that their seniority rights within the professional army were calculated by discounting their years of service before they joined the Quadro Permanente. It was in fact the competition between the milicianos and the professional army officers that led the QP captains to organize themselves in order to press their grievances with more chances of success. The main item of complaint was of course the question of promotion. Those captains for whom a military career had meant escape from their former plebeian environment, and who had nothing to cling to outside the army, neither personal fortune nor family connections, felt endangered. Abandoned by an irresponsible high command, suffering from an acute shortage of modern weapons (so they claimed), unloved by a country that was tired of the wars of attrition, the QP captains realized that even their chances of promotion were now affected. Their opportunities for advancement suffered as a result of the huge injection of milicianos officers. With all their political radicalism, the milicianos frequently belonged to the educated classes, and as military engineers or specialists in advanced technologies enjoyed preferment over the heads of the war-battered, disgruntled QP officers. Nor should the influence of the envied milicianos in the development of political attitudes be discounted. For the milicianos the army was not all they had; quite the contrary was true. They longed to return to Portugal, to their families and civil careers, were disgusted by the war, and turned their disgust into high-sounding Marxist theorizing.

Finally, after more than ten years of inconclusive African warfare nobody among the junior officers any longer believed in those principles of Salazarist ideology that justified their presence in the three rebellious colonies: namely that the Ultramar was nothing less than a cultural-mystical extension of continental Portugal, which was supposed to form a nation-state encompassing Europeans, Africans, Asians, and Indonesians—all of them "Portuguese." A few weeks of active service sufficed to explode this fallacy in the mind of any junior officer. Further, both the QP and the milicianos captains discovered something else as well: the soldiers they commanded, ignorant, often illiterate (in spite of hurried reading lessons given them as recruits), were frequently underfed or showed the ill-effects of malnutrition, and looked to be no better off than the enemy they were sent to subdue, the destitute, illiterate, undernourished African guerrilla fighters. And here the politicized milicianos stepped in: could not both sides, the poor Portuguese peasants and the poor African peasants, be considered as victims of the same financial-political powers? Were not the same monopolies, the same fascist regime, exploiting the masses in continental Portugal as well as the peoples of the Portuguese colonies?

This then was the atmosphere in 1972, when the junior officers of the QP first thought of organizing in order to better defend their interests. However, the actual "Officers' Movement" was formed during July 1973 in Guinea-Bissau. This initiative was a direct reaction to a government decree that permitted the officers of what was now called the "complementary corps" *(Quadro de Complemento),* that is the milicianos, to overtake officers of the professional army (QP) on the promotion list (see Rodrigues et al., 1974; Baptista, 1975). During the meetings in which the thorny promotion list problems were discussed, the captains came to grips with larger issues. There is no doubt that some of the debaters already had a clear view of what they wanted to achieve: a plot destined to overthrow the government. But it was too early to show their hand. The first goal, easily achieved, had been to unify the different groups of disgruntled QP captains in all three colonies and in continental Portugal. Very soon Captain Piteira dos Santos could call for a "promotion list discussion meeting" at Évora, in southern Portugal. In September 1973, during a casual conversation that alluded to every subject possible, the captain touched on the general political problem and said to Lieutenant-Colonel Luís Ataíde Banazol, with whom he was engaged in conversation, that it would be a good thing to free the country, too.[15]

On a farm of the Alentejo province during the summer of 1973, 136 captains and lieutenants went further than promotion list grievances; they decided to take a stand against a government accused of trying to transform the army into a mere praetorian guard of the Caetano regime. At that time it began to be rumored that a right-wing general, Kaulza de Arriaga, had for some time been preparing a coup of his own. Caetano was considered too weak by the "Kaulzaists" who hoped that an extreme right-wing military dictatorship would put more zest in an indolently conducted war. The "Officers' Movement" feared that if Kaulza de Arriaga's plans succeeded, a group of fascist desperados at the helm of the state could destroy Portugal by demanding of it a superhuman war effort. The problem was to outstrip the "Kaulzaists" and steal a march on "the fascist plot." The captains already engaged in their own plotting abandoned the frame of an "Officers' Movement" interested only in advancement technicalities, and were groping toward a name that better expressed their general aims. "Movement of the Armed Forces" (MFA) was finally chosen.

A group of young officers, whose spiritual leader was Captain Otelo Saraiva de Carvalho, busied themselves with elaborating an ideological Marxian program, which was, however, never accepted officially by the MFA. Carvalho, a Mozambique-born Portuguese, who had in the past been friendly with blacks and mulattoes, later engaged in the struggle against Portuguese colonialism. It is quite possible that his own *Weltanschaung* was moulded under the influence of his friend Jacinto Veloso, a Goa-born revolutionary Marxist who later became a leader of FRELIMO, the united anticolonialist movement of the Mozambique insurgents. It was indeed from the FRELIMO that Carvalho took the model of the MFA conspiratorial pattern: small five-men cells, committed to deep secrecy, in which only the cell secretary knew a single member of another cell. But it was from Amilcar Cabral, the leader of the Guinea insurgent movement (PAIGC) that the revolutionary elite of the MFA took its doctrine. Cabral, who was assassinated with the help of PIDE agents on January 20, 1973, had elaborated an original analysis of revolution in an underdeveloped society such as Guinea-Bissau (Cabral, 1971; also 1972, 1973).[16] The gist of it was the designation of the lower-middle class—the petite bourgeoisie—as leader of the revolutionary struggle. This exalted role had to be fulfilled by the lower-middle class in the absence of a self-aware proletariat. There were other reasons too. The lower-middle class had been removed by monopoly capitalism from all economic and political posts of command. It therefore had an axe to grind in fighting against the ruling class (which, in Guinea, was the colonial administration and its local agents). The petite bourgeoisie, moreover, could be considered patriotic enough to identify itself, at least for a time, with the interests of the masses; and as a social stratum as a whole it had sufficient education to organize and lead the revolutionary struggle.

Such an analysis fitted the aims of the MFA vanguard like a glove. The captains were themselves children of that lower-middle class destined for such a lofty historical role. The rest of Cabral's analysis also matched their feelings. The playing down of the working class's place in the process was especially significant. It gave the captains a good social conscience, later encouraging them not to fall under the spell of politicians claiming to speak in the name of the proletariat.

The MFA leadership, besides exploiting patriotic appeals and social idealism, also used more down-to-earth pay increases for junior officers. And the MFA issues, such as profit, led from the political mistakes made by the ruling groups in Lisbon, and there were plenty of errors to exploit. The government, though it ridiculed by its day-to-day policy official versions about a so-called process of liberalization, permitted an opposition congress to take place at Aveiro from April 5-8, 1973. Some weeks earlier, two of the most brilliant liberal intellectuals, the Oporto Catholic lawyer, Dr. Francisco Sá Carneiro, and the Lisbon professor of medicine, Miller Guerra, had resigned from the National Assembly (to which they had been elected in 1969) precisely to protest the lack of liberalization. Professor Guerra, in a grotesque scene, was even prevented by the president of the Assembly from finishing a speech in which he charged the government with preventing liberty of speech. After the government's closing of all constitutional safety valves, there was little wonder that the Aveiro congress, bitter and resentful, adopted slogans inspired by the left-wing opposition. It even went to the lengths of paying tribute to the African leaders of the anticolonial rebellions.

All this was grist to the mill of the secret MFA, and they were unexpectedly helped by a futile gesture of the Portuguese extreme right-wing. The Ultramar Combatants, under the leadership of general Augusto dos Santos, held their convention in Oporto between June 1 and 3, 1973. Elderly ex-servicemen delivered speeches in which the officers on the active list and in combat units discovered gibes at their own supposed lack of fighting spirit. Caetano and his men had no sympathy whatsoever for the Ultramar Combatants, or for the openly fascist "Portuguese Legion" that stood behind it.[17] But the MFA organizers presented the insults hurled against "the army" as a studied indignity offered by the government to thousands of officers. But for the MFA, the Oporto convention was in another sense a gift from the gods. It helped the plotters to bridge the gap that traditionally separated the navy and the air force from the land forces. The MFA organizers succeeded in convincing officers from all three services of the need to join them. There were common meetings, at Évora again; on November 24, 1973 at Oeiras; and on December 1 at Óbidos. Meanwhile the Caetano government had "won" the October 28 elections to the National Assembly. It had been a pyrrhic victory; nobody could take seriously the fact that all 150 seats had again been won by the official *Ação Nacional Popular;* the 66 opposition candidates, complaining of the lack of constitutional facilities to wage an electoral campaign, had all withdrawn from their constituencies on October 25. Caetano prophetically had tried to prevent them from doing so by his ludicrous decree of September 11, which prohibited candidates from retiring before polling day. It had all been in vain. On September 23, some 29 persons were arrested in Lisbon, among them seven opposition candidates, and charged with distributing opposition leaflets, baptized for the occasion "subversive pamphlets." The stand taken by the government impaired its authority among many young officers approached by the MFA conspirators. Official propaganda against Marxist totalitarianism sounded rather hollow in view of the government's obviously totalitarian ways. When, on October 25, a bomb exploded at the regional army headquarters in Oporto (probably a deed of the underground "Revolutionary Brigades"), the feeling was strengthened that only a violent solution could put an end to the crisis. The bomb outrage further encouraged the MFA organizers to press their arguments in favor of a military coup, the only alternative to indiscriminate terror.[18]

In January 1974, the government already knew that something was afoot. But Caetano neglected the warnings. He was even more worried by a menace of another kind: Spínola's book (1974). General Antonio de Spínola, descendant of the famous Genoese family that had done much to help medieval Portugal build its first navies, was born at Estremoz on April 11, 1910. His father was a high official in the country's financial administration. In the course of a brilliant military career, Spinola acquired the reputation of a cunning braggadocio, for which he was "idolized by his subordinate officers." During World War II, he was sent by Salazar as an observer to the Stalingrad front, on the German side of course. It was rumored at that time that his secret reports convinced the Portuguese dictator that Hitler's cause was lost, thus strengthening the country's commitment to neutrality. As commander-in-chief of the colonial army active in Guinea-Bissau, he conducted himself gallantly, personally directing military operations—in glaring contrast to the behavior of many other Portuguese generals. Awarded the highest decoration of his country—the "Tower and Sword"— Spínola created a minor sensation in the interview he gave on September 12, 1969. On that occasion the general berated NATO for not helping the Portuguese war effort in Africa more, sharply scolded the West for not understanding that the Lisbon government had already spent more than two billion U.S. dollars for military expenditure in a cause expressing more than narrow national interests, and he complained of the heavy economic yoke under which the Portuguese people had to labor to back the war effort. The last part of the interview was considered as a covert appeal to public opinion, and as disguised personal political propaganda.

It seems that around that time Spínola lost any hope of a clear-cut military victory in Africa. In September 1973 he was relieved of his post in Guinea and nominated vice-chief of the general staff, headed by his friend Costa Gomes. Even before that date he was already working on his book, *Portugal and the Future,* in which he advocated a "political solution" of the colonial question and the establishment of a sort of Portuguese Commonwealth of Nations.[19]

In November 1973, Spínola informed Caetano that he intended to publish such a book. The prime minister, alarmed enough, asked General Costa Gomes for his opinion. The chief of the general staff answered that his friend's book was "a brilliant service rendered to the country." The book was published in the second half of February 1974. Caetano started to read it on the 20th of the month, could not sleep the whole night, so excited was he by his reading, and closing it the next morning felt that a military coup was by now unavoidable. Spínola had given the rebellious young officers not only the spiritual nourishment they needed, especially the not-yet-Marxist captains, but was lending them his authority and prestige.[20]

The question of a previous link between the MFA leaders and Spinola was heatedly denied by both sides after the coup. But there is no question that such a link existed. The main MFA leaders were in contact with both Spínola and Costa Gomes. At the beginning of 1974 these men had already got themselves transferred to continental Portugal and were completing their preparations. The MFA manifesto was discussed in Vitor Alves' apartment; the first draft had been prepared by him and by Melo Antunes, after being debated by all MFA leaders. The final version—for the time being—was shown to Spinola by Otelo de Carvalho and to Costa Gomes by Vasco Gonçalves. Spínola's many remarks had that "final" version "watered down," at least according to the taste of the more radical military plotters (Expresso, 1975h; Maxwell, 1975b). But in the meantime, plotters of the opposite kind were trying to bring about Spínola's dismissal, and, if possible, even Caetano's. According to rumors, which cannot be lightly dismissed, the aforementioned extreme right-wing general Kaulza de Arriaga, together with some of his colleagues—Silvério Marques, former governor of Mozambique; Joaquim Luz Cunha, acting commander-in-chief in Angola; Henrique Troni, commander of the air force stationed in Mozambique; and others—were explaining to President Tomás that the weak, permissive Caetano government had brought Portugal to the brink of the precipice; only his removal could save the country.

An MFA meeting, held at Cascais on March 5, 1974, gave the green light for further collaboration with Spínola and Costa Gomes. There was no love lost between the sides. The plebeian captains belonged to a different world from the dashing general, great favorite of Lisbon high life. But some of the MFA organizers had fought in Guinea under Spínola and admired his stamina and prowess. Above all they needed each other. Spínola could not dream of playing a central role without the backing of the victors in the coming coup. The MFA leaders could not dream of a successful coup without neutralizing those military units reputed to be already "Spínolist"—the elite 3,300-paratrooper corps, the 3,400 marines, and some motorized units, such as the 7th cavalry regiment.

At the last moment the whole plot nearly came crashing down. On March 14, 1974, the right-wing generals finally succeeded in forcing Caetano to dismiss Spínola and Costa Gomes from their positions at the head of the armed forces. At the Military Academy of Lisbon, surrounded by units of the National Guard, lieutenant-colonel João Almeida Bruno, formerly Spínola's second in command in Guinea, was arrested. In the small garrison town of Lamego, the nervousness at the local garrison reached such a pitch that a loyalist officer threw a grenade at a group of servicemen who, according to him, were dabbling in "revolutionary debate." There was a feeling that a right-wing coup was at hand, or that Caetano was ready to stifle a possible left-wing one. Suddenly, on the night of March 15 and 16, came the news that the 5th infantry regiment had mutinied at Caldas da Rainha, and that an armored column was nearing Lisbon. At three o'clock in the morning, a group of ministers, thinking the revolution had already erupted, fled to the headquarters of the 1st air force command at Serra de Monsanto, which had been chosen as an emergency refuge for the government. But it was a false alert. The Caldas da Rainha captains, mistakenly, had revolted 40 days too soon.[21] Their slender column was stopped at Sacavem, at the gates of Lisbon, by loyalist units, accompanied back to its starting point, and disarmed. Thirty-three officers were arrested, and the government intended to have them court-martialed.

In one sense the Caldas da Rainha incident, which after Spínola's fall from power was ascribed to impatient Spínolists, had been a windfall for the MFA plotters. It helped the officer responsible for the organization of the coup, Major Otelo Saraiva de Carvalho, to check all the weak points of his blueprint. The government, thinking that the mutiny it feared had just fizzled out, was lulled into a false feeling of relief. It is true it was partly disillusioned again by the publication, shortly after the Caldas da Rainha adventure, of a manifesto issued by an unknown body, the "Armed Forces Commission." This document bitterly attacked those superior officers who were participating in the different government meetings and manifestos organized to mark the victory of the regime over the mutineers. It starkly described the "administrative terrorism" let loose by the authorities against officers suspected of having been linked with the *intentona* (failed coup). Three superior officers were given laudative appreciations for their refusal to take part in pro-Caetano rallies: they were generals Costa Gomes and Spínola, and rear-admiral Bagulho. Finally, the Armed Forces Commission declared its full solidarity with the arrested Caldas da Rainha officers, and stated quite openly that the cause for which the vanquished mutineers had fought would in the future be defended "with more precautions taken and with more sense of reality."[22]

For the specialist of the antisubversive activities in the different police services and at the military intelligence headquarters in Lisbon, the manifesto bore the print of unmistakeable communist participation in the plotters' brain trust. But the Caetano government preferred to whistle in the dark; according to the prime minister, the balance-sheet inclined him to optimism. Weighing up the last events at a Cabinet meeting, Caetano complacently stressed that the Caldas attempted coup could have started at all only because the actual commanding officers of the rebellious regiment had been arrested by officers from other units. The loyalist troops had done their duty and the *Lisboetas* kept their calm. Caetano expected the hostile antigovernment forces to try a kind of "remorse revolution," as he put it, in order to free their arrested comrades. In a television and radio broadcast on March 28, the prime minister played down the whole affair, attributing the mutiny to mere *irreflexão* (thoughtlessness, rashness). Caetano warned his listeners that only "foreign interests" could profit from division among the armed forces of Portugal (Caetano, 1974: 245).

III. THE COUP AND AFTER

The plans for the coup, masterminded by Major Otelo de Carvalho, Major Hugo dos Santos, and Lieutenant-Colonel Garcia dos Santos, were destined to bring complete victory by the exploitation of complete surprise.

Underground headquarters were established at the military engineers' barracks at Pontilha. The plotters concealed a concentration of tanks and armor at the Santarém Military School under the appearances of maneuvers. At 11 o'clock on the night of April 24, 1974, a small army of some 5,000 men was at the MFA leaders' disposal, but only hand-picked soldiers and noncommissioned officers. Less than 1,000 were informed that a revolution was contemplated, not a coup. The rebel officers meant it to be not an inner struggle of the ruling class, but an enterprise destined to put an end to the colonial wars and to change the structure of Portuguese society. At 25 minutes after midnight a Lisbon radio station started to broadcast a song by José Afonso, which was the signal given by the plotters inside the capital that everything was all clear. The leadership of the expedition was assumed by 240 officers; 160 sharpshooters covered the column. The insurgent forces occupied the center of Lisbon before three o'clock in the morning. The coup had been timed to coincide with NATO naval exercises, so that the Tagus estuary was free of foreign warships. A ship of the Portuguese Navy, the frigate F-473, whose crew was officered by MFA men, cast anchor off *Terreiro do Paço,* where the major part of the rebel armor was deployed. There was no resistance at all. The Estado Novo crumbled without one army bullet shot in its defense.

In the afternoon a young captain, Salgueiro Maia, went with some armor to the National Guard headquarters and there surrounded the government, which had not even had time to flee to its Serra de Monsanto sanctuary. Caetano refused to surrender to Maia. He did not want, he said, that "the power of the

State should fall into the street." He asked for General Spínola and succeeded in giving his own complete political failure the aspect of a constitutional transfer of power. Spínola, with the mantle of legitimate government thus fallen on his shoulders, was in a better position to impose himself on the victorious MFA insurrection.[23] The only dead of the April coup were the three civilians killed by PIDE agents; these "Gestaportuguese," as the underground press called them, fearing the worst, had barricaded themselves in their Lisbon headquarters, firing indiscriminately into the crowd gathered outside. Major Brito, who commanded the marines ordered to storm the building, had some difficulty preventing a mass lynching of the PIDE agents. But he did, promising that the agents would be brought to justice. From the revolutionary side, the whole coup had been a completely bloodless affair.

The same day the new authorities were constituted, headed by a Junta of National Salvation. Its members were all military men: the generals Spínola, Costa Gomes, Jaime Silvério Marques, Diego Neto, Galvão de Melo; the admirals Rosa Coutinho and Pinheiro de Azevedo.[24] Curiously enough, the MFA leaders had fallen into the background. The efforts to preserve MFA unity dictated this policy of "wait and see." The liberal wing considered that the job had been done, and the army must return to the barracks, letting the civilians build up a democratic regime. The radical left-wing, on the other hand, feared that in a society as conservative as the Portuguese, democracy could never aspire to a West European standard; democracy in the local style could only mean the free but futile interplay of political parties, without real influence on the popular masses—ripples on the surface of an archaic, not even fully capitalistic society. The left-wing of the MFA had not done what it had done to let talkative lawyers restore the bourgeois republic; what the leftist MFA captains and majors wanted was a socialist revolution achieved under their own leadership.

The Junta abolished by decree the institutions of the Estado Novo, promised general elections within one year, announced that the colonies would enjoy the right of self-determination, and appeased Portugal's NATO allies with a declaration stressing their intention of sticking to the country's international commitments. The coup was received abroad with the feeling that such an event had been overdue.[25]

The diplomatic corps accredited to President Tomás, however, appeared to be more surprised. The American Embassy had reportedly not established any prior contacts with the local opposition. According to the same sources, the Central Intelligence Agency station in Lisbon possessed no information of what was happening outside the central Tomás-Caetano cliques, and its main intelligence channel had been the PIDE, so brilliantly outwitted by the young MFA officers (Maxwell, 1975a). It was Spínola who looked for a closer contact with U.S. Ambassador Nash Scott, as the American diplomatic circles had been nearer to the group around Spínola's bitter enemies, Kaulza de Arriaga, Franco Nogueira, Salazzr's former foreign minister and chief ideologist, and the other so-called "integrationists."

After hesitating briefly, the Junta permitted free political activity. Of great—albeit overlooked—importance had been the publication of the MFA program. This document, from which Spínola had succeeded in deleting the more revolutionary passages, still spoke of an "antimonopolist strategy," and these few words were enough to allow any intelligent observer to scent the Marxist inspiration of the authors. But the MFA presence was pushed into the background by the arrival of the exiled political leaders, and the rebirth of party political activity.

The 49-year-old Dr. Mário Soares, secretary of the Portuguese Socialist Party (PS), and the 60-year-old Álvaro Cunhal, leader of the Portuguese Communist Party (PCP), returned from exile, which Soares had spent in Paris and Western European cities, and Cunhal had spent mainly in Prague and Moscow. The former SEDES leaders popped back from "internal exile": Dr. Sa Carneiro and Dr. Magalhães Mota started to organize their own party, the PPD (People's Democratic Party, a left-of-center formation that liked to call itself social-democratic). The sensation of the first days after Caetano's overthrow was the discovery of a strong and active Communist Party, after some 48 years of underground existence. Less than two weeks after the coup there were already some hundred sections of the PCP installed in various buildings belonging to the extinct institutions of the Estado Novo. There was no public power able to prevent PCP activists from establishing their offices where they wanted, as the different police forces were too disconnected and had no authority left. In fact the PCP members suddenly emerging from half a century of suppression seemed to be the only Portuguese to know exactly what they wanted in a society "depoliticized" by the long reign of Salazarism. And what they wanted was to occupy the greatest number of positions of power at the head of institutions suddenly beheaded by the expulsion or arrest of leading Salazarists. Their slogan was *sanear*—to cleanse, to drain, to purify. The MFA program had also promised *saneamento*—sanitation, clearance, clearing-up. With the flag of saneamento unfurled, PCP activists and sympathizers settled themselves on the editorial boards of former pro-government newspapers, at the head of partially State-owned enterprises such as the railways or TAP, the national airline company, and on the management of the national radio and television corporation. *Avante!,* the PCP weekly, which had been printed illegally during the greatest part of the Salazarist era, now appeared in broad daylight, denouncing camouflaged Salazarists and making itself an instrument of party organization as Lenin had indeed asked a revolutionary paper to be.

But the PCP was far from being the only driving force on the left of the Portuguese political spectrum, even if it was the most impressive (Avante! 1974):

TABLE 1
LEADERSHIP OF THE COMMUNIST PARTY OF PORTUGAL

Name	Years of party membership	Years of full time political activity	Years of Central Committee membership	Years of prison under the Salazarist regime
ÁLVARO CUNHAL	43	39	36	13
AMÉRICO LEAL	30	27	from Oct. 1974	2 months
ÂNGELO VELOSO	26	15	8	8
ANTONIO GERVÁSIO	29	22	11	5
BLANQUI TEIXEIRA	30	26	since Oct. 1974	10
CARLOS ABOIM INGLÊS	28	19	16	10
CARLOS BRITO	21	19	7	8
CARLOS COSTA	31	23	14	15
DIAS LOURENÇO	42	32	31	17
DINIZ MIRANDA	28	15	8	12
DOMINGO ABRANTES	20	18	11	11
FRANCISCO MIGUEL	42	39	35	21
GEORGETTE FERREIRA	32	29	21	7
JAIME SERRA	37	27	22	5
JOAQUIM GOMES	40	22	19	2
JOSÉ MAGRO	34	29	17	21
JOSÉ VITORIANO	33	23	7	17
OCTÁVIO PATO	33	29	25	9
PEDRO SOARES	40	22	22	12
PIRES JORGE	40	40	31	16
ROGERIO CARVALHO	27	22	11	15
SÉRGIO VILARIGUES	39	32	31	6
SOFIA FERREIRA	30	28	17	13
ALBANO NUNES	12	9	deputy CC member, May 1974	0
ALDA NOGUEIRA	33	25	17 (deputy)	9
ANTONIO SANTOS	26	16	deputy CC May 1974	12
MANUEL PEDRO	18	9	''	11
ILÍDIO ESTEVES	21	20	(dep.) 9	8
JOSÉ BERNARDINO	18	13	dep. May 1974	7
HORÁCIO JOSÉ	7	4	''	2

The power of the PCP was in its dedicated leadership: a rare group of stalwart revolutionaries who had outlived both Salazar's and Caetano's reigns. They had spent many years in prison, had resisted torture and privation, and in the process, had lost not a few of their comrades, till they emerged through a kind of natural selection process as a unique hard core of Communist Party functionaries. These men and women, generally of proletarian origin, did not, of course, look on the PCP as one of the many parties allowed after April 25 to display normal political activity. For them the Party—with a capital P—was the one and only expression of historical necessity. A socialist revolution realized under PCP leadership was the only normal and necessary development; their own assuming of power was Portugal's manifest destiny. But for the time being the tactic adopted was to back "the heroic MFA captains" and in the eyes of the public to identify the PCP and the MFA, united through the third component of the revolutionary Trinity, the *Povo*—the people, the popular masses.

The PCP had to take into consideration that years of anticommunist propaganda would make it rather difficult for many Portuguese, especially in the northern half of the country, to accept communism as a normal component of public life. The communists therefore encouraged the members of the former Democratic Electoral Commission, a front organization active during the last years of Caetano's dictatorship, to put up a political party under the leadership of a fellow traveller, the left-Catholic professor of economics, Francisco Pereira de Moura. The new body, subsequently called *Movimento Democrático Português* (MDP), was destined to play the role of an auxiliary pro-communist force. It did this in a rather questionable way. In spite of the monolithic appearance it tried to present, the PCP had been torn, in the years preceding the April coup, by a grave internal crisis. In 1963-1964 it was split by the creation of the *Frente de Acão Popular* (FAP), which was headed by a former Central Committee member, Francisco Martins Rodrigues-Campos. The FAP called for resolute combat actions against the dictatorship: did not political power stem from the muzzle-end of a rifle? All the armed groups, which later took part in more or less coherent terrorist activity—the LUAR, the ARA, the *Brigadas Revolucionárias*—were the political offspring of that split. Later, in 1971, a Maoist group crystallized—bitterly anti-PCP—called the MRPP, "Movement for the Reorganization of the Party of the Proletariat," a not-too-subtle hint that the communists were *not* such a party. The PCP, and Álvaro Cunhal personally, took action to prevent extreme-left pressure from growing, but at the beginning of the 1970s communist influence was in decline among students and young workers (but grew among army officers, amidst whom the milicianos represented an older generation of students). Cunhal (1974a) wrote a biting paraphrase of Lenin's "Left-wing communism, an infantile disease" (1920), which the Portuguese leader named *"O Radicalismo Pequeno Burgues de Fachada Socialista"*—"Petty-bourgeois radicalism with a socialist façade." But it was of no avail. However, the left-wing radical revolt would influence PCP leaders after the April coup in a double sense. Cunhal and his friends would try by all means to turn the military power of the MFA against the left-wing radicals, thus shutting them up; and at the same time the PCP would attempt to out-maneuver its too-revolutionary enemies by demonstrating that what the PCP considered the "democratic and national" stage of the revolution, as outlined in Cunhal's "Way to Victory" (1974b), was not just smooth-talking class collaboration. Quite the contrary: the PCP, while struggling through the "democratic and national" stage, would employ methods well-adapted to the next, socialist, stage of the revolutionary process, quite in keeping with the dictatorship of the proletariat. The results of such a tactical choice were soon felt. While there was never the slightest criticism of MFA policy in any PCP declaration, its fire-power was directed at its two main enemies: left-wing radicalism, as already explained; and at the PCP's and left-wing radicals' common foe—the Socialist Party. The PCP tried to outwit both its enemies by a high level of mass mobilization and indoctrination, made easier of course by its control of the means of communication. But its un-doubted knack was to be found elsewhere: in its penetration of the state apparatus, in its seizing control of the main ministries, even if not quite at ministerial level, and in its penetration of the army. The first goal was quite easily achieved by conquering provincial governorships, by assuming power in many municipalities (all of them deprived of their former Salazarist governors and mayors), by organizing the personnel of different ministries, always meekly disposed to serve the masters of the hour. In doing so, the PCP tried, as much as possible, not to put its own men in too-visible positions. It used its small auxiliary force, the MDP, which was promptly dubbed "registry-office for servants, governors and mayors" by ironical observers.

The Socialist Party (PS) was of a very recent creation, in spite of bearing the name of the old socialist party whose seeds were sown a century ago. It had one strong asset—the engaging personality and the powerful oratory of its Secretary General, Dr. Mário Soares—and a strong handicap—the lack of a general staff of working-class background. It was founded as the ASP—the Portuguese Socialist Action—in Switzerland in 1964. Since 1967 its paper, *Portugal Socialista,* had been written in Portugal (illegally), edited and printed in Rome under the supervision of Manuel Tito de Morais, and smuggled back into Salazarist Portu-gal. The fledgling party enjoyed the backing of the socialist international parties in Europe and, in Lisbon, that of the evening daily paper *República,* the most outspoken newspaper in the country. The PS felt strong enough to hold its first convention as a fully organized party, under its present name, in Germany in 1973, and to declare that its ideology was "inspired by critical Marxism" (Portugal Socialista, 1975a). After the euphoria of the first days of liberty, the PS emerged as a socialist party of the European type, with a leadership formed by intellectuals and members of the liberal professions, lawyers, high school teachers, bank officials, and a sprinkling of highly specialized workers, artisans, and fishermen. Later, as the behavior of the PCP and the extreme-left radicals frightened away many workers, there was an influx of proletarian elements into the PS ranks. Soares chose as his party's symbol the raised fist, and rejected the accusation of being "a mere social-democrat"; in the Leninist dictionary that term is akin to "traitor." But the PS stood firmly on the basic principles of representative democracy, as understood in the West. The socialist weekly never tired of explaining that the PS desired, in an atmosphere of "Marxist liberty," to have Portugal "listen to socialism speaking with a human voice" (Portugal Socialista, 1975b). There was very soon a basic misunderstanding between Soares and the MFA officers. He wanted them to return to the barracks as soon as possible and let the working people of the country freely build an open socialist society. One guesses, from PS declarations and from personal contacts with responsible party members, that such a society, of course going an original Portuguese way, would in PS minds have a sort of Scandinavian look to it, but with all enterprises under social control or management. The MFA officers, on the other hand, encouraged by the PCP, became daily more convinced that they must thrust themselves into the corridors of power, behind the scenes. There is no doubt that some of them believed from the first that it would be better to openly assume political power. The PS expectations of establishing a French-style common front with the PCP were brushed aside by Cunhal (incidentally helping cracks to appear in the French "common program" between socialists and communists). When signs clearly showed that PS popularity was growing, PCP attitude towards the socialists crystallized into unrelenting hostility. The PS leadership, taking notice of all the deeds and declarations that proved that Cunhal had no intention of leading his party along the path of "democratic" and "national" revolution, as described in his own *Way to Victory,* hesitated a long time. Finally, when censorship activities and the attempts of the military to stifle the liberty of the press during the summer of 1974 were considered by the PS as PCP-inspired, the socialist position started to take shape. The PS leaders reacted by accusing Cunhal and his friends of aspirations inconsistent with democratic beliefs. The socialists charged the PCP with working to establish a Stalinist people's democracy, complete with political censorship, secret police, and an imprisoned opposition. The PS adopted the slogan "Socialism yes—dictatorship no!" which proved itself well suited to the feelings of the general public. Soares, reminding his audiences of the fall of Allende in Chile, prophesied that if extreme antidemocratic, so-called left-wing forces had their way in Portugal, they would alienate the bulk of the population from socialism. Finally, the establishment of a PCP-dominated people's democracy by force and violence could only provoke new military or other coups, misery, anarchy, and a new dictatorship.

Spínola and a part of the governing junta had turned anti-Caetanist in the past because they considered that Caetano's refusal to break with Salazarism could provoke a leftist revolutionary outbreak. Now that something very like this had indeed happened, the Spínolists tried to dam the flood. Spínola held some trump cards: his personal popularity, the loyalty of a part of the officers' corps, the hope of collaborating with some political parties, and the right-of-center *Associação Programa,* under the leadership of Diego Freitas do Amaral, which would in due time transform itself into the *Centro Democrático e Social* (CDS), financially backed by the main banks of the country. Spínola also hoped to flirt with the new *Partido Popular Democrático* (PPD), a left-of-center party led by Sá Carneiro and Magalhães Mota, the former "legal opposition" to Caetano. The PPD was supposedly backed by the most influential Lisbon weekly, *Expresso.* However, its editor, Francisco Pinto Balsemão, willingly developed a split personality; as a citizen he was a PPD backer, but as an editor he adopted a nonparty objectivity, which together with shiftings in the editorial board for the time being kept the weekly above water in the stormy seas ahead (Expresso, 1975j). There is no doubt that Spínola tried to use both of these parties to consolidate his own power: first the CDS, representing the conservative strata of northern Portugal, and hopefully considered as the most likely to win Church support, in spite of efforts made by an openly Christian-Democratic party to ingratiate itself with the Catholic hierarchy; second, the PPD, an enlightened liberal force, expressing the will of the Portuguese open-minded bourgeoisie and its "technocrats" to democratize Portugal in a Western sense so that it could make sufficient economic progress to join the European Economic Community (EEC). Jumping on both these horses Spínola hoped to ride the storm, establishing a presidential regime "as in the United States," leading the colonial empire along a very long decolonization process, with a Lusitanian Federation as its final goal, and accepting sufficient structural changes to put the country on the same level as France concerning the relative weight of nationalized enterprises versus private ones. At that stage Spínola was still working hand-in-glove with General Costa Gomes, who, on May 6, told a press conference that the ruling junta had only one function, and a limited one to boot: the restoration of democracy.

The PCP and its allies in the MFA leadership could not accept the idea of ending military rule. They were determined to preserve it when the first legal and civil government, presided over by Professor Adelino da Palma Carlos, assumed power on May 16, the day after Spínola had been sworn in as provisional president of the republic. The general thought it wise to invite both PCP and PS leaders to take part in the government. He hoped to use the PCP to hold down the salaried classes and to entangle communists and left-wing radicals in a deadly struggle, and expected to exploit the socialists' international relations to improve Portugal's position in the world. During the presidential inauguration at the royal Queluz palace, Spínola mused about the return of his country to the fold of democracy after almost half a century of dictatorship. When political minorities are allowed to impose their will on the majority, he said, the power of the State turns always into tyranny.

IV. DAYS OF AMBIGUITY

Professor da Palma Carlos, 69 years old, a rich business lawyer, had a political past in the anti-Salazarist opposition, but he looked down on the overthrown dictatorship from a purely constitutional point of view: Salazar had been wicked to liquidate representative democracy. As former dean of the Lisbon law faculty, Professor da Palma Carlos had not shown great concern for social issues transgressing the legal field. As head of government he saw his first duty as "normalizing" public life. This meant, in fact, establishing a legal basis for Spínola's wished-for presidential regime. At a certain moment the prime minister found himself in an objective tactical alliance with PCP leader Cunhal; both wanted to postpone the election promised by the MFA program. Palma Carlos desired this, as the organizational tools for a triumphant Spínola election were not yet ready. Cunhal backed the prime minister on this particular issue, because with all democratic parties allowed to compete, the electoral prospects of the PCP looked rather dim. Palma Carlos' government included 14 ministers: three communists or procommunists (Cunhal, Labor Minister Pacheco Gonçalves, MDP's Pereira de Moura), the first and the last without portfolios, as they both wanted to dedicate themselves to tasks of party organization; three socialists (Soares of Foreign Affairs, Salgado Zenha of Justice, and the Minister for Social Communication and Information, Dr. Raul Rego, editor of *República;* two PPD (Magalhães Mota of Interior, Sá Carneiro, without portfolio); the rest of the Cabinet was center-left. All were civilians with the exception of the Minister of National Defense, Lieutenant-Colonel Firmino Miguel, a Spínola man.

As some "constitutional satisfaction" had to be given to the leading MFA officers, a Council of State was appointed and sworn in on May 31. The new institution comprised the seven members of the Junta of National Salvation, seven nonparty dignitaries (university people, but also a center-right politician,

Freitas do Amaral, and Lieutenant-Colonel Almeida Bruno, by then head of Spínola's military household), and seven members of the MFA Coordinating Committee, who were destined to play a role of first importance in the coming string of crises. Of these, Colonel Santos Gonçalves, Major Vítor Alves, and Major Melo Antunes were the most prominent.

The Salazarist regime had left its democratic successor a heavy economic burden to bear. After almost half a century of dictatorship, whose justification had been the need to liquidate party quarrels in order to let the country concentrate on basic economic problems, Portugal was the poorest country on the continent (with the exception of Turkey, a country with only a toehold in European territory). Portugal was the last country in the field of dwelling units per 1,000 inhabitants (4.3). Similarly, Portugal was also behind in telephone ownership (78), cars (60), electricity consumption (770 w); only in the owner-ship of television sets was the record of Greece even poorer than that of Portugal (38). Tax evasion was a national sport of the affluent. The coming loss of the colonial empire would hurt industries working for export, which were perhaps sufficiently equipped to produce goods acceptable to the African consumer, but could not dream of sales on the European market. Since 1966, Portugal had been unable to redress its balance-of-trade deficit. On the eve of the coup it had reached 1.2 billion U.S. dollars (OECD Economic Survey, 1974; Der Spiegel, 1974b: 82). Between March 1973 and March 1974, the rise in the cost of living—which had been 7.2 percent in Germany, 9.7 percent in Switzerland, and an impressive 15.7 percent in Spain—reached a record 30 percent in Portugal. In 1974 the gross national product of Portugal, on a per capita basis, was still at 730 U.S. dollars, lower than that of Spain (1,100 dollars), Italy (1,860), or France (3,360); it was somewhat higher than the GNP of Iraq (428) or Brazil (421) (OECD Economic Survey, 1974; Der Spiegel, 1974: 82).

The Palma Carlos government granted all wage-earners a minimum salary of 3,300 escudos a month (half of the workers' demands) and took measures to freeze monthly salaries higher than 7,500 escudos; however, it conceded textile workers a 4,300-escudos salary, and lost its credibility. Lacking political cohe-sion, the Palma Carlos cabinet showed itself unable to adopt a coherent line concerning both labor demands and larger economic issues.

Prompted by their own misery, but visibly encouraged by groups of the extreme left, industrial workers from the Lisbon and Oporto regions pressed for a minimum of 6,000 escudos per month, a 40-hour work-week, and the dismissal of managers, executives, and even private industrialists who had served the fascist dictatorship. The last demand was a studied infringement of ownership rights. Very soon the country was engulfed in a gigantic wave of strikes. The strikes were absolutely opposed by the PCP, furious at seeing its own lack of authority over the working class so noisily demonstrated. Cunhal was behind the attempts to curb, by force if necessary, the CTT strike in June (and the TAP work stoppage in August, under the next government). The Portuguese could admire the strange spectacle of the communist leaders going along with the industrialists. Owners of industry announced their willingness to pay higher salaries and to lessen their profits; sufficient unto the day is the evil thereof. But it was a feast of left-wing radicalism; its leaders, if one is to judge their aims by reading their declarations, felt themselves equal to making the journey to utopia.

The greatest outburst had been that of the 7,000 workers from the LISNAVE naval construction yards. They asked for a more thorough purge of Salazarist personnel than the first PCP-organized *saneamento* had produced; and demanded workers' control of the means of production. In defiance of police orders, the LISNAVE strikers traversed half Lisbon and noisily demonstrated their anger in front of the Ministry of Labor, a communist ministry. A "Defense group of the Lisbon and Setúbal metal workers" violently attacked Palma Carlos' government and denounced PCP and PS ministers for their "betrayal of the working class." The bitter enmity of *Avante!,* the PCP central organ, toward the strikers gave to a "Solidarity Commission with the struggle of the Textile and Woolen Goods workers" the pretext to publish, on May 21, a declaration bitingly critical of those communists and socialists who preferred sitting with Palma Carlos in the same government to fulfilling their proletarian duties (V. J. Silva, 1975).

The utopian left-wing radical leaders even tried to induce workers to institute "self-management" in locked-out enterprises, a scheme fought by the PCP as "anarchist" but willingly accepted by the salaried—maybe less by the power of a messianic vision of "libertarian communism" than by a normal desire to be their own bosses. At the stationer's firm Dominguez & Lavandinho, one of the biggest in the country, which for different reasons was nearing bankruptcy, a steering committee of shop assistants was elected by the general assembly of employees, and the extreme left-wing papers announced that "real socialism is at hand." A wondering American professor, Curtiz Todd Darling, in a study destined for the *Daily Californian,* described the attempts of the cooks and waiters of the *Cova da Moura* restaurant to organize the new managing committee. For people of whom the most educated had attended school only up to the fifth form, it was an uphill task. The cooks and waiters were, however, helped by educated members of the extreme left-wing terrorist group LUAR. Both the PCP leaders and the MFA officers looked upon these social experiments with deep distaste. Self-management smelled too much of Titoism (a term still dangerous for old-fashioned revolutionaries), of left-wing radicalism, of "effete reformist socialism." The PCP and the MFA were united in their love of order, discipline, uniformity, and subordination (V. J. Silva, 1975; Ferreira, 1975).

The Palma Carlos government had inherited a very difficult agricultural situation. The long-term stagnation of the country's agricultural output, which had been a major drag on the national economy, had not been ended, as Salazarism had boasted. Small improvements in one sector had been paid for by detrimental processes elsewhere. Especially grave were the social problems in the Alentejo provinces. The *latifundia,* the quasi-feudal *senhores'* way of life, the vast and growing hunting grounds, the widening gardens, and the huge private *quintas* (farms) with their large dependencies, tended to transform the granary of the country into a steadily growing game preserve. Areas of nonagricultural exploitation, cattle-ranching, and abandoned, unprofitable land, made the life of the peasants hard and unrewarding. On the eve of the coup, a permanent exodus of inhabitants, affecting both High (Alto) and Low (Baixo) Alentejo, with the exception of a narrow strip along the relatively industrialized Setúbal coast, was both the result and the further cause of a steady process of depopulation and impoverishment. The people leaving the south-eastern quarter of Portugal were active, able-bodied men and women. In 1974, 61 percent of the remaining active population was aged less than 20 and more than 60 years—the bulk of people between 21 and 59 having joined the near-million Portuguese condemned to look for work in France, Germany, Luxembourg, and Belgium. The number of persons active in the agricultural sector declined during the decade 1960-1970 in the main Alentejo districts, without any compensation in the growth of local industry. For all those years the southern half of the country suffered from lack of water. The Salazarist irrigation projects were so slowly realized that the fresh quantities of water made available were consumed by the population and could not in many cases be put to agricultural use. The combined results of all these weaknesses increased emigration. Portugal was the only country in Europe with a declining population. The Mértola district, for instance, between 1960 and 1970 lost no less than 40 percent of its inhabitants (Santos and Bagulho, 1975). The left-wing radicals found in the Alentejo fields congenial ground for activity. They tried to organize the agricultural workers and even incited them to burn down the harvest to exert pressure to obtain a rise in their salaries. The PCP took it badly, as it considered the Alentejo region its own political domain, having established cells of salaried peasants back in the 1950s. The left-wing radicals were accused by the communist press of playing the role of fascist stooges. The period of communist participation in the Palma Carlos government was indeed one of poisoned relations between the PCP and the different leftist groups, and this state of affairs affected their future disagreements, becoming a permanent feature of recent Portuguese political history.

But another event was to confirm not only the ubiquitous presence of the MFA leadership (quite beyond its official participation in office, controlling as it did, 33 percent of the Council of State membership), but also the warm collaboration between the victors of the April 25 coup and the PCP against a common foe. It was the birth of their common child, the Press Regulation of June 21, which again imposed restrictions on the press, after less than two months of complete, Western European style liberty. The regulation, announced as intended to "guarantee the liberty to express ideas," actually forbade incitements of strikes, offending the government and the Council of State, publishing "false news"; and, most importantly, it prohibited "ideological aggression." This last item covered anything that criticized and prevented the application of the

MFA program, that had as one of its aims the liberty of the press. Penalization followed immediately. On July 3, two evening papers—*República* and *A Capital*—were heavily fined for covering the arrest of army officers who had refused to help break a strike. Other papers were suspended. Three publications, the evening *Diário Popular* and two weeklies, *Sempre Fixe* and *Expresso,* withheld publication as a sign of solidarity. But things went further. One of the most anti-PCP left-wing radical leaders, José Luis Saldanha Sanches of the MRPP Central Committee, was arrested on June 7. The weekly he edited, *Luta Popular,* was suspended "indefinitely," accused of "insulting and criticizing" the MFA and Spinola. *Revolução,* organ of the RPR (Party of the Revolution of the Proletariat), suffered a similar fate. At the same time revolts broke out on editorial boards against the supporters of the former regime. At the *Diário de Lisboa* the former strong man, Lopes Souto, was *saneado* (purged); at the *Diário Popular* events were more or less the same, as, with variations, at *O Século* and *Diário de Notícias;* but profiting from the purge of Salazarists, groups adhering more or less to the PCP tried to take the control of the editorial boards. At the *Diário de Lisboa,* when a motion was carried protesting the June 21 Press Regulation, there were already rumblings by PCP men who denounced the protest as "reactionary and regressive." Together with their MDP allies, the communists, helped by their MFA sympathizers, systematically gained control of the Lisbon and Oporto press. The papers did not become more interesting as a result. Together with the MDP commissars, dullness entered the editorial boards. *Diário de Notícias,* which enjoyed a relatively big circulation of 79,000 papers a day in March 1974, fell to a dismal 32,000 a day in December of the same year, after being "made progressive." Jean-Paul Sartre defined the new Portuguese press as "a lump of official communications and political statements." The June 21 Press Regulation and the consequent "conquest" of the editorial boards by the PCP-MDP-MFA trinity gave the Portuguese press its present characteristics, described by a Lisbon journalist (H. V. de Silva, 1975) as "a deep lack of imagination, a sad lack of humor, a distressing routine, and, to crown it all, a relative incompetence." Only the *República,* The SP-inspired evening paper, with its fine antifascist record, belonging to a multitude of small share-holders, stayed unconquerable among the dailies for a number of months. With the radio and television network things were made easy for the MFA. On June 14 the Cabinet nominated Lieutenant-Colonel José Calvão Borges, a distinguished air force officer, as president of the state broadcasting corporation; but even before the nomination the MFA leaders were already interfering with the programs. On June 10, Vice-Admiral Rosa Coutinho appeared on television to explain why a certain satirical program would not be broadcast. And so it went.

The collaboration between PCP (with its MDP appendix) and the MFA officers celebrated its honeymoon during the Palma Carlos government, which finally brought its downfall. The MFA men, wanting to follow "the way of a national and independent socialism," felt of course flattered seeing a political force as ancient and as revolutionary as the PCP, with all its power, sticking to them. At the first stage, when many politically naive young captains met a communist speaking only about "friendship," "comradeship," and "gratitude to our heroic captains," these expressions were willingly accepted as worth their sentimental content. The more mature MFA leaders stayed flattery-proof. But one of the PCP articles of faith was readily swallowed by the MFA rank and file: the one about the wickedness of the PS and its leader, Dr. Soares. For those war-tempered officers, for whom softness was anathema, it was vital to explain that the PS was "reformist," and that reformism meant softness and lack of punch—in a word, cowardice. Could Soares himself, speaking so many foreign languages, on such friendly terms with social-democrats all around Europe, really be considered a stalwart Portuguese revolutionary? It should not be forgotten that the driving force behind the MFA was made up of officers, most of whom were born after the establishment of Salazar's dictatorship. They had never read a free newspaper, never listened to the proceedings of a debating society, never learned to take barbs directed at their convictions humorously. When they were still orthodox Salazarists, the other side was wickedness itself, satanical communism; after turning into ardent "military revolutionaries," the armed builders of socialism decided that whoever was not willing to embrace the same views must necessarily again be wicked. Of course the MFA leaders understand what social and economic interests mean: that was the reason for their more lenient stand toward the PPD, the party of the petite bourgeoisie, the artisans, and the small land-owning peasantry in the north of the country, then towards the SP, which is a party of salaried people, workers, and employees. Having no other economic interests to defend than the workers backing the PCP (with the MDP appendix), many among the MFA did not understand why the Socialist Party took a position so different from the Communist Party, which never criticized the MFA. This is also the reason for the rough treatment meted out to some extreme left groups when they attacked in speeches and writing the David and Jonathan of the Portuguese Revolution, the MFA and PCP. This alliance was to show itself very effective in bringing down the Palma Carlos government.

The prime minister had been unable to put an end to the gathering wave of strikes. The whole fabric of Portuguese society, after some 50 years of imposed stagnation, "looked like an active volcano," as a LUAR leaflet put it. The government failed to meet its June 27 deadline, the day it had set for publication of permanent legislation on trade union affairs and strike regulations; as PCP and PS ministers had opposing views on this question. The PCP wanted a strong, unified, centrally organized, and communist-dominated trade union, for obvious reasons; and the socialists desired, as in France, a regime with a pluralistic syndical system. The government was paralyzed.

But there was more: Palma Carlos—and probably Spinola behind him—felt very uneasy having to govern with the MFA program as a unique constitutional text. He desired either a return to the 1911 republican (and very democratic) constitution, with the addition of indispensable changes, or the working out of a provisional constitution. Also frightened by the number of governorships and mayoralities occupied by the procommunist MDP, especially in rural areas, Palma Carlos, quite out of touch with reality, thought that the peasants of northern Portugal would be influenced, and tried to postpone the elections at least to 1976. His opponents could thus charge him with being afraid of democracy; the PS ministers, who knew better in which direction the wind was blowing, were—on the contrary—eager for general elections within the first year of the new regime. The pro-Palma Carlos attitude of the PCP in this matter has already been alluded to.

At the same time, tension was growing between President Spínola and the MFA leaders. The first dispute flared up around the Mozambique problem. Against the swift decolonization plan presented by the MFA's Major Melo Antunes, who asked that foreign minister Soares be ordered to act in accordance with its directives, Spínola preferred quite another scheme of things, which was dubbed the "Procrastination Plan." He wanted to nominate in the colony a man faithful to himself. The discussion ended with a MFA officer, Vítor Crespo, being sent as high commissioner for Mozambique. The most serious clash between Spínola and the MFA leaders occurred in June 1974. The occasion was, again, a meeting convened to study ways of accelerating the decolonization process. The officers complained that with Palma Carlos the whole affair would "rot for years," which the MFA could not permit since they saw the colonial question as the crux of the matter. Without a swift solution of that problem, no radical changes were possible in continental Portugal.[26]

It was not only Palma Carlos' leadership that was worrying the MFA officers. In the ruling Junta there were elements considered dangerous, both for their "reactionary" ideas and because they had the potential to gain a popular following. One of them was General Carlos Galvão de Melo, young, ambitious, and already flirting with the right-of-center CDS. The general showed himself to be very articulate on television. Without mincing his words, he called the regime under which the country was living "a carnival democracy," and alluded darkly to "witch-hunts." Tact was not his forte. Galvão de Melo chose to deliver one of his scathing attacks on Portuguese affairs during a visit to Brazil, and it was considered in bad taste even by the MFA's adversaries. Other indiscretions convinced the MFA that Galvão would never become "a second Spínola." Soon the left concluded that this possible enemy did not have "the abilities to realize his potentialities" (Expresso, 1975m).

It was against the background of a broadening conflict between Spínola and the MFA members of the Council of State that Prime Minister Palma Carlos tried to take the initiative in presenting the government with a set of wide-ranging proposals. He proposed presidential elections to be held within three months, a course of action that could enthrone Spínola as the head of the state for years to come. At the same time, on July 5, Palma Carlos asked the Council of State for wider powers in order to deal with problems made insoluble by the contradictory views held by his ministers. The Council accorded him some minor satisfactions, but under MFA influence brushed away his main proposals, whereupon the prime minister resigned on July 9.

Events proved that Palma Carlos had not worked alone when planning a strengthening of his executive powers: Three ministers, in solidarity with him, presented their resignations. They were Vieira de Almeida (Economic Coordination), Magalhães Mota, the PPD leader (Interior), and Spínola's faithful Lieutenant-Colonel Firmino Miguel (National Defense). During the crisis the stand taken by the MFA members of the Council of State, who had rejected Palma Carlos' proposals, was extolled to the skies by the communist press. After the prime minister's resignation, *Avante!* criticized him for wishing to liquidate "the indispensable coalition nature" of the government, which meant that rightly or wrongly the PCP believed that Palma Carlos would have used his widened powers to dismiss the communist ministers.

During the last days of the Carlos cabinet, and during the following interregnum week, the MFA leaders observed with misgivings how President Spínola had ordered troops to be moved into Lisbon and to occupy positions around the capital. It was proof that the MFA did not yet effectively control the armed forces. Actually the victorious captains had tried to extend their sway upon military units that had never had any connection with the April coup. A Spínolist senior officer, Jaime Silvério Marques, had been engaged in preventing MFA emissaries and "enlightment groups" from influencing various regiments, and he would continue his activity also after Palma Carlos' fall. But for the MFA leaders the question of controlling the whole Portuguese army was a vital one. They tried, in speeches and interviews, to convince the general public that "the Movement of the Armed Forces is identical with the armed forces on the whole." However, with Spínola at the helm no radical purge of the higher military staff was yet possible. The MFA leadership turned this difficult corner by creating, on July 12, the "Commando for Continental Portugal," COPCON for short, which was to grow into a group of military companies with some 5,000 men. It included picked volunteers, the best shots, the best signals material (NATO stuff), the best light armor, and the strongest (per capita) fire power of the entire army. In theory the supreme commander of the new force was General Costa Gomes, head of the General Staff and then still Spínola's friend. In fact the actual commanding officer, Otelo de Carvalho, former head of psychological warfare services in Guinea-Bissau, turned out to be the strongest man in the country. A popular, bantering "soldiers' favorite," Carvalho was promoted on the spot to the rank of brigadier and appointed military governor of Lisbon.

The COPCON did not tarry in becoming, as its own officers readily admitted, "a revolutionary organ." With Carvalho turning more and more to the extreme left, the COPCON started to act "more in the spirit of common sense than in the frame of formal legislation." It was sometimes a law unto itself, and had the means of enforcing it. As the authority of the traditional police forces faded away, COPCON took upon itself the task of public guardianship, in the spirit of Carvalho's conceptions. In conflicts, disputes, or acts of violence with social or political undertones, the COPCON would always act on behalf "of the masses"— even if the right, as understood by "bourgeois law," was with the other side. For many destitute Portuguese COPCON appeared as a *santa milagreira,* a new holy miracle-wonder. For a part of the left-radical movement, it was "the motor of the political process," "the nerve center," the main link in the MFA-*Povo* symbiosis ("the popular masses"). The PCP was less enthusiastic. Carvalho would loudly report and prevent acts of PCP members and sympathizers that conflicted with public order as understood by COPCON. Otelo—soldiers called him by his strange Christian name—had stated proudly that the men under his command would see that Portugal should not become "a satellite of imperialisms," with a stress on the final *s,* which meant that in the COPCON commander's eyes the Soviet Union was no better than the United States. He used to add that the country should neither be "a bourgeois democracy" nor "a party dictatorship," another veiled allusion to the PCP (see Note 26). On the other hand the tendency of the new task force to dabble in political police matters would bring with it a less flattering reading of its initial letters: *Como Organizar PIDE Com Outro Nome* (How to organize PIDE under another name), and that not only in right-wing circles. In any case the transformation of COPCON into a military-political police would awaken in its commanders' minds a better understanding of the former PIDE, three months before still their arch-enemy. An astonished public would read in the best-seller Carvalho found time to write that the hated and despised PIDE agents had been, after all, "only state functionaries, fathers of families, earning a living for themselves and theirs like anyone else" (Maxwell, 1975a). This could only mean that a MFA leader was laying claim to the Movement of the Armed Forces' right to establish a new political police. The seed, COPCON, had already been sown.

V. BIDS FOR POWER

The second provisional government of the renovated democratic republic, formed on July 17, 1974, differed from the first one not only in having seven officers in ministerial posts of a total of 17 government members. It was the first to get an MFA prime minister, Colonel Vasco dos Santos Gonçalves. This "Savonarola in uniform" had behind him a double career of officer and private contractor.[27] From 1955 he had served in the defunct *Estado da Índia* at Goa, and in 1966-1967 in Mozambique; it was in Angola, where he had been in 1970-1971, that the futility of the colonial war clearly appeared to him. Among the MFA leaders, he was a driving force. The public thought him a moderate, somewhat lukewarm leftist. In fact Vasco Gonçalves found himself hand-in-glove with the PCP. His rise to the premiership was a triumph for the procommunist wing of the MFA. The efforts of President Spínola to get his protege Firmino Miguel nominated prime minister had ended in failure. The difficult discussion that preceded the formation of the new government gave the MFA the opportunity of proving its political hegemony over the country, and that was guaranteed by the guns of COPCON.

A curious fact about the second provisional government was the illusion it gave of socialist ascendency. Compared with the single PCP and PPD ministers (Cunhal and Magalhães Mota, both without portfolios), the PS disposed of four ministries: Soares kept Foreign Affairs; Zenha, Justice; the well-known historian Magalhães Godinho received the National Education Ministry; and Antonio de Almeida Santos, more openly identified with the PS, kept the Ministry of Interterritorial Coordination, an "ashamed ministry of the Colonies" that had not much sense left in the summer of 1974. Most remarkably, the Ministry of Labor had been taken from the PCP and given to an MFA man, Captain José da Costa Martins; but that did not mean that the communists had fallen from grace with the Movement of the Armed Forces. The PCP did not care to keep a ministry that made it vulnerable to the attacks of the extreme left and of the working population and preferred to let an officer take it. Two ministers were Spínola's faithful: Firmino Miguel, responsible for Defense; and Major José Sancho Osório, the minister for Social Communication (Information). Both represented the ghost of a living reality: guns and radio, tanks and newspapers— that is, "Defense" and "Social Communication" belonged not to the incumbent ministers, but already to the MFA-PCP alliance. During the stormy night meetings at the Council of State, when the formation of the new Cabinet had been discussed, it had become apparent that the real seat of power was not any more in the government, and not in the Council, but in the COPCON-backed MFA leadership, which called itself modestly "the Coordination Commission." The Commission had brought into the new Cabinet two of its men, Majors Vítor Alves and Melo Antunes, as ministers without portfolio, to let them learn the ministerial trade (Melo Antunes would soon inherit Foreign Affairs from socialist Soares). Spínola was whistling in the dark when in his July 18 speech he tried to present the new Cabinet as established according to his own wishes. He even promised that the new Gonçalves government would restore "discipline"—that is, put an end to the revolutionary process. But having lost so many positions of power, Spínola and his friends knew that the president's popularity was still unimpaired among the peasantry and in many sections of what his rivals called "the popular masses." In the two-and-a-half months left to them they would wager everything on that "silent majority"—and lose.

Having had their way, the MFA leaders and ministers made the solution of colonial problems their first priority. Even tactically it was a wise political choice. It united MFA, PCP, PS, most of the PPD, and part of the extreme-left fringe, and isolated the Spinolists. But it was characteristic of the political level of the Portuguese bourgeoisie, highly depoliticized after living in the Salazar and Caetano hot-house for so long, that it did not understand the historical moment Portugal was living through and was incapable of uniting in defense of its interests.

According to usually reliable sources, a group of prominent right-wingers tried to organize themselves, not with the aim of helping Spínola but in order to fight him and his followers. For the "savage extreme right" Spínola was a traitor, ready to abandon the *Ultramar* and its natural treasures. Among the anti-Spinolist right-wingers were figures connected with the struggle behind the scenes against Caetano: General Kaulza de Arriaga, a board member of *Petrangol*, the Angolan oil concession; Admiral Sarmento Rodrigues; and Franco Nogueira; Salazar's minister of Foreign Affairs and executive head of interests connected with the Espírito Santo banks.[28] But Spínola's removal could only play into the hands of the left, united on the colonial issue.

This left feared, above all, not the fossilized generals and politicians who were in any case under COPCON surveillance, but the conclusion of an alliance between the Spinolists and the partisans of Portuguese supremacy in the colonies. As Carvalho claimed later, such an alliance had been in the offing. Spinola was of course seen as indirectly responsible for a series of events that stressed the power and influence of right-wing circles, and that were regularly described as "provocations" in the PCP-MDP-controlled press. The revolt of PIDE agents, detained in a Lisbon prison, who complained of being harshly treated, was interpreted as a sign of "encouragement from above." When police forces tried to repulse young demonstrators clamoring for "a people's judgment" and "a revolutionary tribunal" for the PIDE men, some of the crowd were injured (August 12). A much graver attack by the National Guard on a left-wing demonstration during the night between August 14 and 15 resulted in a fight during the course of which a young man was killed. On the top of all this, the news, received on August 20, that the minister of the army in the last Caetano Cabinet, General Alberto de Andrade e Silva, together with the leader of the "Portuguese Legion," Francisco Casal Ribeiro, were to be set free, added fuel to the anti-rightist press campaign and public meetings (Diário de Lisboa, 1974b, 1974c; Diário de Notícias, 1974a, 1974b, 1974c; O Século, 1974d).

Particularly irksome to the Gonçalves Cabinet were the multiple activities of a Portuguese millionaire from Mozambique, Jorge Jardim, mayor of Beira. A former Salazar minister and friend of Caetano, Jardim had been received by Spinola on May 4. This man, who in 1972 had equipped, at his own expense, an entire regiment of black paratroopers destined to fight the Mozambique FRE-LIMO guerrillas, was suspected by the MFA "of plotting against decoloniza-tion." Jardim's role as Malawi Consul-General in Beira was annoying enough; but the backing he received from Malawi, a black republic, in activities suspected of leading to Mozambique's partition was unbearable to Lisbon. The "Jardim affair" led to the breaking-off of diplomatic relations between Portugal and Malawi on July 23, the initiative being taken by the Gonçalves Cabinet (Daily Telegraph, 1974).[29] Even worse for the Lisbon government were the rumors about the "Independent Front of Occidental Continuity" (FICO), a white people's organization in Mozambique. In Portuguese the initials FICO mean "I Stay." It was feared that links had been established between Spinolists and FICO, and with an armed group of white ex-service men calling themselves the "Death's Dragons"; the aim of this "reactionary collusion" was to stop first decolonization in Africa and then "democratization" in Portugal.

General Spinola did nothing to soothe the qualms of the MFA leaders who suspected that he would stick to the "Commonwealth ideas" expressed in his book and oppose full independence for the colonies. So, for instance, in a speech delivered on August 7 he made no bones about his disagreement concerning the union of the Cape Verde Islands with the future republic of Guinea-Bissau. From a liberal-constitutional position such a statement could not be attacked; as the population of the islands had not been consulted by elections or referendum, the Lisbon government had no right to hand them over to the PAIGC, the Marxist-Guinean *guerilleros* movement. Spinola knew that in the Cape Verde islands the

Democratic Union, under the leadership of João Baptista Monteiro, was fighting the proposed union with Guinea-Bissau (Diário de Lisboa, 1974a). But on the other hand, the PAIGC leaders, MFA's favorite colonial revolutionaries, claimed the islands as a part of their future state. Spínola's stand was considered detrimental to decolonization, as were his later personal attempts to negotiate with President Mobutu of Zaire about the future of Angola. The outbreak of grave disturbances in Mozambique was once more linked by left-wing MFA leaders to "reactionary circles" in Portugal—a euphemism for the president. In fact, the white rebels—who on September 7 seized the main broadcasting station of Lourenço Marques and the local airport—were protesting the signature, the same day, of the Lusaka agreements with the FRELIMO by Portuguese representatives (Foreign Minister Mário Soares, and ministers Almeida Santos and Melo Antunes). The Lusaka protocol promised to FRELIMO that on June 25, 1975, all of Mozambique would form a single republic under its sole leadership. The MFA left wing was appalled by the passivity of the troops and officers in Lourenço Marques, who had given the rebels a free hand. The news that Salazarist officers had left Portugal to take command of the "Death's Dragons" and of the FICO (which in happier times they would have considered just "white trash") led the left MFA to believe that there was more in those events than met the eye: a plot (The Times, 1974a).[30]

But if a plot it was, it had been poorly organized: two MFA officers, Major Duarte Costa and Lieutenant-Colonel Dias de Lima flew to Lourenço-Marques, and their influence was sufficient, together with the lack of hoped-for-external aid, to thwart the "Death's Dragons"; the FICO revolt crumbled three days after having come very near to proclaiming unilateral independence (The New York Times, 1974).

It was a remarkable success for the Lisbon regime, and it was followed on September 10 by another conspicuous advance of its policy: the granting of formal recognition to the new Republic of Guinea-Bissau at a ceremony in the Belém palace, the president's residence. Many observers thought that this triumph of decolonization was the turning of the tide. But the same day President Spínola warned the left wing of the MFA and the government: in a televised speech, postponed several times, he finally spoke his mind. A huge rally in his support was convened in the name of the "Silent Majority," against "the totalitarian extremists active in the shade" (República, 1974). It was a declaration of war against the extreme left.

The main Portuguese cities were slowly flooded with green posters calling citizens to participate in the pro-Spínola rally: the posters showed a human head having, instead of the mouth, the words "Silent Majority." Left-wing vigilantes tore them up by the thousands, but the day after the walls were again plastered with the green man without a mouth. Ad hoc committees sprung up in residential neighborhoods to help organize a legal mass demonstration, which was nonetheless attacked daily in the press and in broadcast commentaries as if it had been a dark conspiracy concocted in the underground.

The MFA with its left-wing allies did not really fear a rightist coup; for against COPCON, armed to the teeth, it had no chance. It feared that such a mass rally would give President Spínola the political legitimacy they lacked.

The left-wing parties had been active during the preceding weeks organizing elections to "freguesias" (city districts) committees, which were commissions of citizens charged with vague tasks of supervision and "social help"; these elections were a golden opportunity for the PCP and its small MDP ally to put to use their well-oiled political apparatus. PCP-MDP candidates presented themselves under their own party labels, but also as representatives of "fishermen's wives," petty artisans and shopkeepers, or the "working population of the district" —both in Lisbon and Oporto. These committees, packed with PCP front men, took upon themselves the task of marshaling the population in the lower parts of the capital against the pro-Spínola rally, which was to take place on September 29. Alarming press reports were published about "fascists" trying to smuggle in arms and landlords setting up airfields in their Alentejo domains in order to get reinforcements "from abroad" (presumably Spain). Rally-day was presented in the PCP-controlled press as a future Saint Bartholomew's Night of all "decent democrats." But the left still had not a case against a public manifestation called to express sympathy to the head of state; the lack of political maturity shown by the Portuguese right was to furnish the elements of that case. On September 26, the president of the Republic, accompanied by Prime Minister Gonçalves, was warmly acclaimed at the Campo Pequeno, the Lisbon bullfight arena; at the same time the prime minister was hooted at. The revolutionary tunes played by the orchestra met with derisive shrieks. The cry of *"Viva o Ultramar!"*—long live the colonial empire—was enthusiastically cheered. Outside the arena, the mounted National Guard scattered a pro-Gonçalves manifestation. It was no more than a storm in a tea cup, but in the excited political atmosphere it provided the political *casus belli* the left had been looking for against the advance of Spínolism and its supporters (Expresso, 1974d, 1974e).

The next day, September 27, the government discussed without coming to a conclusion whether the pro-Spínola manifestation was to be authorized. The president's men in the Cabinet, Defense Minister Miguel and Information Minister Osório, stated that a ban would be illegal. But it was already too late. PCP-MDP leaders, aided this time by left-wing radicals willing to bury the hatchet in order "to fight the bourgeoisie," together with the communists mobilized their forces. The *freguesias* committees carried a motion asking Spínola to prohibit the pro-Spinolist manifestation. Three reasons were given: nobody knew who was financing the rally; everybody knew that "fascists" were taking part in the pro-Spínola ad hoc committees; there had already been acts of violence. Neither names were given nor actual happenings mentioned. The railway workers under PCP or left-radical influence announced that trains carrying people to the pro-Spinolist manifestation would not be allowed to proceed. Trade unions appealed to their members, asking them to prevent the pro-Spínolist crowds from entering Lisbon by road (O Século, 1974c). These measures were sufficient to paralyze the rally organizers.

The Spínolists tried to fight back. Defense Minister Miguel ordered the National Guard to occupy the broadcast stations. Information Minister Osório went on the air announcing that the rally would take place at the appointed hour. By that time, however, COPCON forces, coming to the rescue of the communist and left-wing radicals, started to set up road-blocks at the gates of Lisbon, and searched vehicles heading for the capital. President Spínola, incensed by the news, ordered troops he thought loyal to guarantee free access to the city. These orders were not obeyed, as the regiments considered to be Spínolist had already been penetrated by pro-MFA and pro-left "enlighteners." In a last effort, the president of the Republic, in his capacity as supreme commander of the armed forces, summoned both Prime Minister Gonçalves and COPCON Commander Carvalho to the Belém palace. They were held there under de facto arrest until four o'clock in the morning, September 28. By that time the presidential palace was surrounded by COPCON troops and the two MFA leaders were released. Immediately upon Carvalho's release, COPCON proceeded to arrest supporters of the former regime (Expresso, 1974f).

Spínola convened the Council of State, trying to have it back his proposal to declare a state of emergency. Such a measure would have given the president the right to seize military installations and to order the arrest of the MFA leaders. But General Costa Gomes, chief of staff, opposed the demand. It was a turning point, as cooperation between the two men had hitherto been smooth. It was also the end of Spínola's presidency. At noon, September 28, he was prevailed upon to ban the "Silent Majority" demonstration that he had sponsored 18 days previously. Spínola resigned two days later, but not without broadcasting a Cassandra-like speech; the outgoing president prophesied economic chaos, and charged the PCP with sabotaging democratization.

Costa Gomes was nominated president of the Republic the same day, and the three Spínolist members of the Junta (Generals Galvão de Melo, Jaime Silverio Marques, Manuel Diego Neto) were dismissed by the MFA. There were two developments that, although buried in the back pages of Portuguese newspapers, were highly significant: when PCP chief Cunhal attacked the defeated Spínola, charging him with attempting to stage a reactionary counter-coup, and describing him as a self-seeking opportunist, President Costa Gomes reacted promptly: he ostentatiously invited the former president to dine with him in one of the best restaurants of Lisbon. In spite of the new president's popular nickname of "cork," earned by his ability to stay on top whatever the political situation, he left nobody in doubt about his own oppositions to extremism. There was also a statement delivered by Major Vítor Alves, minister without portfolio, to the press (October 3): after all, there had been a plot, but it had not been engineered by Spínola; "reactionary elements" had tried to assassinate, during the stormy September 28-29 weekend, both Spínola and Premier Vasco

Gonçalves (Expresso, 1974g). It is true that the Salazarist old guard had never quite forgiven Spinola his "betrayal," and Spinola, even after losing power, even after fleeing Brazil, did not forget to mention that the responsibility for the "chaos" had been, above all, Caetano's.

When Costa Gomes was proclaimed president of the Republic, the PCP staged a huge demonstration in his honor, in which thousands of "Lisboetas" (and apparently also admirers imported from provincial towns) marched to the Belém palace. The PCP did it mainly to achieve two aims: to show that the communists did not even bother to ask for a permit for a mass rally, which had been denied to the "Silent Majority"; and to demonstrate that the PCP had the following necessary to fill the streets—incidentally turning all central Lisbon into one gigantic traffic jam—and that it could do so furthermore without the help of other left-wing parties. President Costa Gomes invited some privates to stand by his side, in order to demonstrate that this was no manifestation of a "personality cult." Several days later the new president stressed that the army did not seek to revenge itself on the defeated Spinolists, adding that it preferred to return as soon as possible to its military duties (Der Spiegel, 1974a). It was a view shared by the moderate, partly PS-inclined wing of the MFA leadership. But the sharpening of the political issues gave the extreme left wing the feeling that it was better qualified to express its views on Portugal's future.

The COPCON command pointed to the links between the organizers of the "Silent Majority" affair and certain right-wing press organs such as *Tempo Novo* or *Banderra* and right-wing parties such as the Portuguese Nationalist Party, the Liberal Party, and even the fascist-minded Progress Party—all of them closed or banned after Spinola's resignation. COPCON officers also announced that at the headquarters of the Progress Party—Avenida Infante Santo no-65 in Lisbon—their soldiers had unearthed 200 tommy guns, 100,000 cartridges, 100 machine guns, 100 automatic pistols, 2,000 rifles, and 50 howitzers. The trails led to where the left-wing press had predicted: to the business and banking interests of the Portuguese bourgeoisie—neither the middle class nor even the upper-middle class, but a moneyed ruling group nursed, pampered, and coddled by nearly half a century of fascist rule.

Portuguese economists (Moura, 1962; Pinto, 1958; Pintado, 1964) had drawn attention to the anti-liberal character taken in Portugal by capitalism, which elsewhere had led to liberalism. In fact, the country's rulers themselves were fond of making fun of the lack of initiative of Portugal's capitalists, if not prompted by the political leadership. Caetano in exile wrote with bitter relish, carefully choosing his words, about *"a prova mais provada da incapacidade da iniciative privada em Portugal"*—"the most proved proof of the incapacity of private initiative in Portugal."[31]

There were some monopolistic groups that supported Spinola for the simple reason that decolonization carried out too rapidly would have affected their interests. One of the main ideologists of colonialist Salazarism, Dr. Franco

Nogueira, a brilliant essayist and Salazar's Minister of Foreign Affairs, was chief administrator of the Espírito Santo group, which controlled vast domains in Africa: pulp paper in Angola, beer interests in Angola and continental Portugal (a near monopoly of production and sale), and petroleum (again in Angola of course). Other examples could be given to point to the "sentimental link" between moneyed interests, political power, and Portugal's seaborne empire.[32]

Under Salazar; a distinguished professor of economics, the Lisbon government had hoped that as a result of the benefits heaped on the monopolistic groups, they would help the economy to "take off." In fact, immediately after World War II, with most of Europe devastated, Portugal's economy presented a pleasant, almost prosperous image. Salazarism was not able to reduce the real gap between Portugal and West Europe. Despite population growth and economic development, Portuguese society remained basically rural; but agricultural production under Salazar went through cycles of stagnation or decline. Private capital was invested in the colonies, not in the backyard sections of the domestic economy. Per capita income remained about one-quarter lower than in Spain, the poorest in Europe (OECD Economic Survey, 1974; Der Spiegel, 1974b: 82). These facts must be borne in mind if one wants to understand present-day Portuguese attitudes, rural, urban or military: as much as the great majority of the population recoils from a new dictatorship under left-wing sponsorship, there is no sympathy for the local brand of capitalism, which failed to fulfill its "historical mission" of the modernization of Portuguese society.

The Espírito Santo group, which invested so heavily in Angola, had its main strength in Portugal in a string of banks and in the Tranquilidade insurance company. This was not much of a contribution to industrialization; in fact Salazar's ambiguous attitude towards industrialization together with his integrationist-imperial mysticism made it easier for Portugal's super-rich to invest in the Ultramar, neglecting the continental fatherland. Salazar, who had been born in a small town, feared that the triumph of industrialization would bring with it the rise of a powerful socialist movement. He preferred the traditional exchange of local raw materials (cork, fish, wine, citrus fruits) for foreign manufactured goods to go on indefinitely, and praised the simple, pure life of the nonindustrialized areas.

But at the same time, the ambiguity of the Estado Novo and the ambivalence felt toward capitalism on Caetano's part did not prevent other powerful economic groups from growing up: there were real monopolistic empires, such as the Champalimaud's complex, containing such banks as the famous Banco Pinto e Sotto Mayor, insurance, paper industries, tourism, the monopolies of steel and cement—which controlled heavy industry, shipbuilding yards, private and governmental housing projects—and the inevitable stock-ranching in Angola. It is true that after the April coup the "emperor" himself, Antonio Champalimaud, the industrialist closest to President Spínola, tried to work with the new regime; but as he naturally asked to be given special protection by the new rulers ("in the interest of efficient large-scale production"), he was setting limits to decolonization; this could not be accepted even by the PPD, let alone the PS and the MFA-PCP alliance.

Besides Espírito Santo and Champalimaud there were two other giant economic empires. The Quiná interests included oil in Angola, data processing, newspapers *(Diário Popular, Jornal do Comércio,* in part the Oporto *Primeiro de Janeiro),* fishing, textiles, civil construction, tires, large interests in southern Africa, and three banks: Borges e Irmão, Banco Crédito e Industrial, Banco do Alentejo. The biggest of all was the Melo fortune (the *Companhia-União Fabril,* CUF), which had the highest profit margins in Europe, a record that impressed Wall Street and the city more than the CUF employees. The Melo family owned nearly 10 percent of the total share capital invested in all of the companies in Portugal. It appears that the tobacco monopoly was at the root of this huge interest complex, but around it sprang up some 186 enterprises, highly diversified, from restaurants, tourism, real estate, insurance, refining, cellulose, and mining to textiles, chemicals, fertilizers, and, crowning it all, huge shipbuilding enterprises. CUF's stockholders' equity the year before the coup was almost 537 U.S. dollars and its assets at least two-and-a-half billion dollars (Maxwell, 1975). These huge interests were dominated by some 100 families and directly controlled by an even narrower circle of 20 families.

These were the multimillionaires who owned pre-revolutionary Portugal. They had the technical know-how, but the long period passed in the Salazarist hot-house had done much to blunt their political finesse. They were trapped by the events without quite understanding them, like the French nobility at the time of the Revolution. Some of these "first families"—Champalimaud, Viana, Santos, Fonseca—fled, taking their money with them. Other representatives of the Melo, Espírito Santo, and Palmela stayed long enough to give the COPCON the opportunity to arrest them. It was, all told, a peculiar set of very rich people. They never gave a thought to philanthropic foundations; they never brought forth democratic-minded scions as other very rich families in Western countries had done. Haughty, selfish, "they were never even kind to one another" (Cal, 1975). The biggest and almost unique cultural foundation of some standing in the country, the *Fundação Calouste Gulbenkian,* was given to the nation by the will of an Armenian multimillionaire. The Portuguese millionaires were not interested in culture and charity.

But—and here one meets the specific facet of local sectarianism—the PCP and the other left-wing radical groups never directed their fire against this small, hated, and vulnerable set of the super-rich people. This would have been in accordance with the pre-revolutionary program prepared by Cunhal, and in harmony with the "antimonopolist strategy" promised by the first MFA manifesto. But it would also have involved the PS and the PPD in a vast "antimonopolies front"; both the socialists and in a certain measure the social-democrats had always held that only the abolition of the privileged position enjoyed by the big monopolistic economic empires would contribute to the country's modernization. The concentrated fury of the communists was directed against the PPS and the PPD, as if these parties represented the multimillionaires' interests. Some reasons could be given to explain such tactics.

After Spinola's fall the analysis of the crisis convinced some MFA leaders that presiding over "the revolutionary process" without taking direct part in it would put the Movement of the Armed Forces on the wrong track: that of a passive observer to a PCP takeover. The MFA leaders felt the need "to institutionalize" their power and up to the fall of 1974 the PCP had gladly accepted the slogan "MFA-Povo," symbolizing the "unity between the armed forces and the popular masses." The PCP looked upon itself as the embodiment of the popular masses, and supposed that the conquest of the MFA from the inside would not present major difficulties; the blueprint of the revolution's final stage seemed to appear crystal clear. With the transformation of the MFA into a political institution, the apotheosis of PCP-directed "revolutionary processes" had to be postponed; thus the PS and its leader, Dr. Soares, became the main enemy of the MFA and the PCP, as the socialists were absolutely opposed to a PCP takeover and more than lukewarm to any political institutionalization of the military leaders.

But the Spinola crisis brought to light some very instructive facts about the operative power of the PCP in the Lisbon area. The well-oiled PCP apparatus filled the MFA officers with awe. It had been able to paralyze the planned-for demonstration before it started and it had shown itself capable of organizing the "popular control" of Lisbon's gates before the COPCON got the idea to do the same. Indeed, the PCP was too strong for comfort, and the MFA leadership started to pick up its political counsellors in left-radical groups far less powerful, as the MES (Movement of the Socialist Left); Carvalho, who was not too happy to see the PCP playing a role he wanted monopolized by his own COPCON, began a political flirtation with another left-radical group, the PRB-BR (Revolutionary Party of the Proletariat-Revolutionary Brigades). In view of these developments both PCP and left-wing MFA leaders could preserve their alliance, which was still considered profitable to both sides, only by having a foe to fight together. The Socialist Party was an excellent common enemy even though Dr. Soares never ceased to affirm his friendship for both PCP and MFA and to stress the socialists' will to build with them a pluralistic socialist democracy.

Immediately after the inauguration of Costa Gomes as president, the efforts of the MFA leaders toward organizing themselves into a coherent ruling framework accelerated. The result was a three-tiered pyramidal structure. It featured on top a 20-member Supreme Council composed of the president of the Republic, chairman by right, the leftover six members of the Junta of National Salvation, the six officer-members of the government, the COPCON commander, and the seven members of the MFA Coordination Commission, one of whom acted as secretary at the meetings of the new institution that were scheduled for every Saturday.

The second tier of the structure was formed by the MFA General Assembly, composed of delegates elected by the councils of the three services: the army (land forces), navy, and air force. The General Assembly meetings were held on the fourth Friday of every month under the auspices of the 5th Division of the General Staff.

At the floor level of the "institutionalized" MFA were the basic councils of the three services. The Land Forces Council, for instance, numbered 114 delegates, of which 45 were elected, 31 were appointed, and 38 belonged by right, as members of the military hierarchy. The elected deputies were sent to the Land Forces Council by the different military regions according to their numerical importance (ten from Oporto, five from Coimbra, seven from Tomar, seven from Evora, and sixteen from Lisbon). Those who belonged to the Council by dint of membership in the military hierarchy included the representatives of the Land Forces in the Junta, four members of the General Staff, ten men representing various departments inside the service, and others; with some numerical differences, the army and air force councils were essentially the same (Expresso, 1974a). Without realizing it, the Portuguese revolutionary officers were trying to construct *mutatis mutandis,* a twentieth-century version of Oliver Cromwell's New Model Army.

The fall and the early winter of 1974 gave the other main political forces of the left—the PCP and the PS—the opportunity to call the roll of the faithful and hold their national conventions. The communist *congresso extraordinário* was a solemn affair. In his opening speech on October 20, Alvaro Cunhal gave his definition of the "dictatorship of the proletariat." Dictatorship in Marxist terminology, contended Cunhal, means the domination of a certain social class and nothing else. Therefore, in Portugal the dictatorship of the proletariat, in which the working class and its allies control the state power, can take various forms. It can assume even the form of political pluralism, expressed in the existence of various parties *("ditadura . . . pluripartidária").* It was regrettable, admitted Cunhal, that the term "dictatorship of the proletariat," which means "a regime more democratic than the most democratic of all bourgeois democracies," uses the same word with which the Portuguese people described the tyranny of Salazar. But, he argued, an unfortunate case of homonyms would not compel the PCP to change its basic concepts.

Three slogans illuminated the convention hall as well as the future tactics of the PCP: "Unity of the Working Class," which would soon be translated in an attempt to thrust all trade-unions under the roof of the PCP-dominated *Intersindical;* "Unity of the Democratic Forces," which would inspire the communist effort to eliminate both PS and PPD from public life; and "The Strengthening of the Alliance Between the People's Masses and the MFA." The latter slogan meant exactly what it said, if PCP is substituted for "people's masses." The Communist Party had decided to stay close to the MFA officers who held the monopoly of public physical power in Portugal.

It should not be assumed too quickly that the above-mentioned slogans represented proof of hypocrisy and double-dealing on the part of the PCP faithful. Stalwart members of the party accepted Cunhal's analysis as gospel. They could not understand, let alone accept, the arguments of trade-unionists unwilling to be regimented in the PCP-controlled *Intersindical,* or of self-avowed left-wing socialists who claimed to be fighters for a new, free, socialist Portugal despite their rejection of Cunhal and the PCP. They considered such arguments blasphemy, holding it to be axiomatic that without acceptance of the leadership of the PCP there is no salvation for the working people and "the honest intellectuals." Persons denying that leadership by definition abjure membership in the working class, the democratic forces, and the people's masses. The PCP slogans thus do not apply to them.

At the same PCP convention, the participants listened to good tidings about the growth of their own strength. Cunhal announced that the membership of the party had doubled between June and September 1974. He identified 60 percent of the PCP members as workers and 18 percent as employees. Nothing was said about the social origin of the remaining 22 percent, and no aggregate figures were given (Avante!, 1974).

The tactics adopted by the PCP did not uniformly please those throughout the world communist movement. *Pravda* published commentaries in the same spirit as the PCP pronouncements, along with hostile remarks about the PS (Ermakov, 1975). But the Italian and Spanish communist leaders made clear their distaste for the PCP line (Le Nouvel Observateur, 1975a, 1975b; Bianchi, 1975a, 1975b). In France, Cunhal's tactics and statements produced sharp tensions in the electoral alliance of communists and socialists (Expresso, 1974b). The feedback of these negative reactions provided ammunition for the Portuguese Socialist Party.

The PS national convention, in the late fall of 1974, was a far less solemn affair than the PCP conclave. Yet, it made up for it in flamboyance, as various currents in the party clashed head-on.

The PS majority, led by Soares and Marcelo Curto, had to close ranks in order to fend against attacks from the right and from the "activist-revolutionary" wings of his party. Soares, in his programmatic speech, emphasized the possibility of building a free, democratic, and socialistic society in Portugal, which he saw as the collective desire of the mass of salaried people and small artisans. The tone of his speech radiated optimism, because he knew already what the MFA leadership and the communist central committee knew as well: namely, that secret and in fact illegal (prohibited by the army) samplings of public opinion had indicated victory for the socialists in the coming elections. Opening the convention with the slogan "Hail Socialism in Liberty!" and closing it with "Long Live the Socialist Revolution!" Soares was able to defeat a social-democrat countered motion by a group led by Sousa Tavares and supported by some well-known personalities. Soares countered the motion in a speech in which he characterized social democracy as useless for present-day Portugal, going so far as to accuse it of the sin of sustaining capitalism.

Soares had more difficulty in countering the utopian fringe led by a romantic, anarchist-Guevarist revolutionary, Manuel Serra. Serra, who mistakenly believed that general elections would not be held, had gained the sympathy of some noted socialists such as Arons de Carvalho, Tito de Morais, and Antonio Macedo. When he was defeated, he tried to split the party by walking out. Yet, the splinter group he took with him quickly disappeared into limbo.

The statutes adopted by the socialist convention differed sharply in spirit from those of the communist conclave. Very little was said by the socialists about central authority and discipline, and much about the need for decentralization and "basimo"—denoting permanent contact with the grass roots of the party (Expresso, 1975k). Many delegates at the PS convention had voiced their fears regarding the future of free speech and free press in Portugal. In fact, among all the newspapers in the country only several were still independent from MFA control or PCP-MDP subversion. *República*, the old courageous antifacist and prosocialist evening daily was the next prominent target.

The assault against the independence of *República* was heralded already in November 1974. An article by the paper's editorial writer, Antonio Reis, that criticized the transformation of the MDP into a full-fledged political party offended the sensibilities of the compositors and printers, and they refused to put the article into print. Everyone knows that the MDP—Portuguese Democratic Movement—is a front organization of the Communist Party, and even the latter has taken no pains to hide that fact. Thus the printers of *República* inaugurated their tactic of selective "strikes" against the publication of articles that did not please the PCP Central Committee. In this way the PCP tried to dictate the political line of a paper that backed the PS.

The tactic was not limited to newspapers. PCP-inspired printers refused to print Caetano's *Depoimento* (Deposition) in spite of the green light given by President Costa Gomes, and although the book could easily serve as a moral and historical bill of indictment against the exiled author; they also refused to print Solzhenitsyn's *Gulag,* which contained not a single word about Portugal. It was easy to divine who stood behind Solzhenitsyn's boycott by Lisbon's printing-shop workers. Of course, officially no responsible body could be pinned down. A Press Council constituted by the decree 85-C/75 of the Provisional Government was functioning, manned by a judge, three officers, six journalists, two representatives of the press (one of them being Francisco Balsemão, editor of *Expresso*), and the delegates of the four coalition parties: PCP, MDP, PPD, and PS (Expresso, 1975a). The Council, however, showed itself to be powerless against "the will of the workers."

An eeriness reminiscent of Kafka's novels pervaded the whole discussion about the liberty of the press. The Press Council, which had the official duty "to safeguard" that liberty "from interferences by the political and economical powers," was sympathetic to the plight of the press. The other political parties besides the socialists were also sympathetic, at least in theory. The MFA was sympathetic. But any press items even mildly critical of the PCP and its allies could be printed only at great pain, if at all. Editors and commentators were forced to adopt a tongue-in-cheek style that could be grasped only by the discerning few: it was a return to the practice under Salazarism, when *República* more than once had succeeded in smuggling to its readers antiregime news and commentary under the noses of Salazar's censors. Alarmed by the growing intolerance of self-appointed censors in print shops, editorial boards, and radio studios, the Portuguese writers rang the alarm signal. Toward the end of 1974 the best known authors and journalists signed a declaration upholding the right to enjoy "uncompromisingly" the liberty of expression. Among the 58 signers were the world-renowned historian A. H. Oliveira Marques, the poets Sophia de Mello Breyner, Michael Torga, and many other notables. Signature 48 was that of Raul Rego, the editor of *República* (Avante!, 1975a).

Among the fiercest fighters against the liberty of the press, and against all other "formal" liberties, were various shades of the left-wing radicals who constituted a formidable presence in the Portuguese streets, at least until election day. They were both vocal and active in the seedy quarters of Oporto and Lisbon, where they impressed young workers, the growing number of unemployed, and to a certain degree also, the underworld. They represented nothing new in the political landscape of the country: in the twenties, the "Red Brigades" and similar groups were responsible for the disorders and the bloody events that weakened the First Republic and paved the way for the colonels who brought in Salazar. The strength of the radical left lay in their tactics of concentration in the most vulnerable spots of industry and society. It was the radical-left nucleus, active at the huge Lisnave shipyards, that stirred up thousands of workers, especially the younger ones, against PCP hegemony (an action that led to the removal of the communist Minister of Labor). Similar groups urged unemployed and destitute slum dwellers to take over the new houses in which many other workers, emigrants in France and Germany, had invested their life-long savings. The left-wing radicals counted no more than several thousand members and they were split into more than a dozen warring factions, but their agitations were enough to produce a nightmare for the orthodox communists. For the PCP, left-wing radicalism—the children's disease of communism, as Lenin had put it—represented the incapacity to analyze a given situation in order to define a clear political line, the hurry "to pass stations without stopping in a headlong haste to establish socialism when conditions are not yet ripe," and a childish cult of violence (Caetano, 1974: 52, 77). The PCP condemned the *esquerdistas* (left-wing radicals) as *agents provocateurs* in the service of fascist bourgeoisie or petite bourgeois students. Actually they were dangerous competitors for the communists, especially in surroundings where young workers were numerous, and their contemptuous criticism of the Soviet Union maddened the PCP.

Yet, there was some truth to the charge that many *esquerdistas* were students. As the universities had been practically closed, some 28,000 idle students furnished idealists ready to dabble in revolutionarism. But the PCP accusations were rejected by the left-wing radicals, who maintained in many leaflets that they were actually ready to use violence only in good earnest and knowingly; violence, after all, was only an answer to bourgeois rule that represented permanent violence against the masses. The pamphlets abounded with other flaming statements: bourgeois laws, by definition unjust, need not be obeyed; justice, being always class justice, must not be respected by the wronged class. Armed with such principles, the left-wing radicals represented a rather disquieting force of "revolutionary fighters." They had enjoyed their hours of glory under the Salazar regime, when the ARA (Revolutionary Armed Action) had committed "antifascist outrages" in the port of Lisbon; when an anarchist group had put fire to the São Domingos church; when the LUAR (League of Unity for Revolutionary Action) had attacked the Air Force base at Tancos, destroying planes and helicopters; and when, to finance the revolution, the LUARists had robbed the Figueira da Foz branch of the Bank of Portugal (Expresso, 1975i; Semprun, 1975: 53). The communists feared especially the MRPP, which had called upon the Portuguese soldiers to desert and to put the weapons "at the service of the people." Both the PCP and the MFA kept a wary eye on the MRPP's plotting in the armed forces; they feared the influence this extreme radical group might gain among the soldiers. The group did make some converts among the soldiers of RAL, the Light Artillery Regiment. When the MRPP organized a rally to protest the arrests of its members at Alcoentre, Tires, and Santarém, RAL soldiers were sent to prevent the demonstration from nearing the São Bento palace, the prime minister's residence; yet, they permitted their MRPP comrades to transform the vast esplanade in front of the palace into a kind of Hyde Park (Expresso, 1975n).

Besides the MRPP, there was a gaggle of other radical revolutionary splinters. The FSP (Socialist Popular Front) was directed by the romantic revolutionary Manuel Serra, who, as has been mentioned, had tried to split the socialist party. The UDP (Democratic Popular Union) was led by Afonso Dias, who saw his movement as "a fish-bone stuck in the bourgeoisie's throat." The PUP (Party of Popular Unity) saw democracy, parliamentary and representative, as "a bloody road leading back to fascism." The LCI (Communist Internationalist League) looked upon anything left of the Socialist Party as purely fascist. The FEC (Electoral Communist Front), a more recent creation, shared with the MRPP the crown of martyrdom in that its members had been subjected to "limitations of activity" by MFA authorities, after assertions that the Portuguese workers were tired of patronization by the army (an attitude officially described as "provocation of confusion and indiscipline") (Expresso, 1975l).

The PRP-BR (Revolutionary Party of the Proletariat-Revolutionary Brigades) represented a more impressive *esquerdista* group for three reasons. First, it

Assembly, asking those who were going to the polls to cast blank ballots. Second, it was led by two "professional revolutionists" of some standing: fattish Isabel do Carmo and black-bearded Carlos Antunes. Finally, the PRP-BR was widely suspected of influencing the political thinking of General Carvalho, COPCON commander. The PRP-BR considered elections nothing more than a camouflaged bourgeois-imperialist coup. It urged that the PS be liquidated just as the Russian bolsheviks had liquidated the socialist parties after the 1917 Revolution. The country, it argued, must be led by "revolutionary councils" composed of workers and give its faith to those MFA leaders "who are revolutionary to such an extent that they are able to go with the working class 'till the end'." The Portuguese army must be reconstructed and composed in the future of armed workers in plants and industries, soldiers of working class background, and revolutionary officers. One aspect of the political conception held by the PRP-BR made it unique in the radical-revolutionary spectrum: namely its absolute faith in the purity of COPCON's revolutionary mission. PRP-BR leaders criticized the other left-wing radical movements that did not share this faith, stressing that never had COPCON men behaved but in the interest of the toiling masses. The PRP-BR militants were fond of reminding of cases in which COPCON had taken a stand contrary to the position of the MDP civilian governor of Lisbon (Carvalho was his military counterpart). Particularly in the seizure of houses for the benefit of the poor COPCON had always manifested, to quote Isabel do Carmo, "completely revolutionary behavior" (Expresso, 1975o).

More complex was the stand of the MES (Movement of the Socialist Left), a sophisticated group with intellectual leadership. MES wielded influence among those radical MFA officers who found the PR-BR too utopian and the PCP not inspiring enough for people seeking their own, independent road to the socialist future. In flat contradiction to the other left-wing radical groups, MES did not parade its disdain for intellectuals. On the contrary: one of its main luminaries was a first-class historian and publicist, César Oliveira. MES had taken over from the last century's local revolutionary tradition a strong dose of anticlericalism, sprinkling its publications with phrases about the "heartless and greedy clergy." Founded in 1970 under Caetano, MES had the unique privilege among the left-radical movement in claiming its right *not to be* a Leninist party. It was also opposed to the general elections for the Constituent Assembly. The main enemy, for MES, is "big capital." At the same time, the Movement deems nationalization of private enterprises a worthless endeavor as long as the working class will be unable to control production; in the absence of such control, argued the MES pundits, no socialism is possible, but only a rigid state-directed bureaucratized apparatus. MES was sharply critical of PCP actions in the trade union arena, particularly the communist tactic of seizing control of trade unions through the votes of small, unrepresentative, and contrived "general assemblies of workers." The PCP's behavior was characterized by MES leaders as "party opportunism"— the exploitation of the low political level of the proletariat, with little regard for

Marxist principles or ultimate consequences of such cynical manipulations. MES exhorted the education of workers and suspected the PCP of wanting to domineer over the working class (V. J. Silva, 1975).

The main forces of the Portuguese left strayed into a contradiction from which there was no exit. The contradiction took the form of a twisted syllogism:

All social progress and social justice is borne and expressed by the toiling masses. We are for social progress and social justice. Therefore, we shall not permit the toiling masses to express themselves.

With the exception of the PS, all the left-wing parties were either unhappy about the coming elections or opposed to them. Before the elections, another discussion focused attention upon the problems of democracy versus socialism. It has been mentioned that the criticism of the MES leaders had been directed at what they described as PCP manipulations in trade-union affairs. The *Intersindical* affair permitted to the whole of the working community to fix its ideas on the subject.

Under Salazar free trade union activity had been barred as a criminal offense. Accepted by the authorities were only the stifling structures of the corporative Estado Novo; this system placed workingmen's "unions" under the supervision of the employers' federation, the state authorities, and the police. Under the stress of reformist demands, Caetano's government, eager to transform the obsolete Salazarist Estado Novo into a new look—*The Estado Social*—permitted a slight democratization of the official structures. As a result, a handful of communists, clandestinely organized, succeeded in occupying key positions in trade unions. The different unions thus captured maintained clandestine contact, helping one another to fulfill the directives given by the underground PCP. But the Caetanist inspectors insisted on the strict separation of unions in accordance with the finest shades of every craft; thus, joiners, carpenters, and industrial wood carvers were not allowed to flock together in the same union, even if they worked in the same enterprise. The aim was to prevent common action.

After the April coup, Portugal's workers discovered with bewilderment that suddenly there was a central trade union body, called Intersindical, for which many of them had never voted. The Intersindical and the PCP that controlled it went directly to the top, asking the MFA leadership to decree that there be one and only one trade union central in the country. The socialist trade unionists asked for a kind of referendum in order to ascertain if all of Portugal's workers indeed wanted to be forbidden to organize themselves in as many syndical bodies as they wanted, according to the French model (CGT, CFDT, FO, and so forth). But the PCP warned the MFA officers that if they did not accept the principle of "uniqueness" of a trade union high command, the workers would not be controlled, and chaos would follow. To the workers the PCP trade gained visibility when it decided to boycott the elections to the Constituent unionist explained that, as the class struggle unifies the working class, it is only logical that local tactics should be integrated into a unified strategy determined by the Intersindical. Both socialist and left-radical activists pointed to the Intersindical project as simply applying to the Portuguese scene Stalin's theory about the need to reduce trade unions to the simple role of conveyor belts to the workers of the directives of the party.

At a stormy assembly of workers, held in Lisbon on December 22, 1974, the adversaries of the Intersindical project were physically expelled from the hall. Finally, the Supreme Council of the MFA decided on January 21, 1975, that the PCP-backed (and initiated) Intersindical monopoly project should be the law of the land. It was a close vote of 11 against 9. But the whole discussion had so excited and frightened the vast working-class public about the dictatorial tendencies of the PCP that it was another pyrrhic victory for the followers of Alvaro Cunhal (Ministry of Mass Communication, 1975). These vague storm signals notwithstanding, the MFA in late 1974 was still in an optimistic and even triumphant mood. Up to that time the revolutionary officers had felt that public opinion was in their favor, reflecting the people's gratitude for their liberating role and the achievement of some of the goals the MFA had set for itself. These included a national minimum wage that, even if considered too low, had benefited about half the industrial and service workers and about 68 percent of civil servants. Pensions for retired and disabled persons had been increased by over 100 percent, reaching a monthly minimum of 1650 escudos. The end of the colonial wars had permitted the government to plan a reduction of 40 percent in military expenditure for the next year's budget. The allotment to public health registered a rise of about 40 percent over the last year of the former regime, and that to public education a rise of over 50 percent. But it was also true that an inflation rate of nearly 30 percent gnawed at much of these increases.

In the field of foreign policy the successes of the new Portugal had been even more impressive. In addition to the recognition of the Republic of Guinea-Bissau and the Lusaka Agreement with FRELIMO (The Mozambique Liberation Front), which included the setting up in Mozambique of a transition government until June 25, 1975, the MFA government had taken four important steps toward decolonization. In Algiers, an agreement between Portugal and the Liberation Movement of São Tomé and Principe Islands was signed, also establishing a transition government until the granting of full independence, in July 1975, was reached. In Lisbon a similar agreement was signed with PAIGC (the African Party for the Independence of Guinea and Cape Verde) regarding the independence of the Cape Verde Islands in July 1975. In January 1975, the Algarve Agreement between Portugal and the three warring Angolan movements (MPLA, FNLA, and UNITA) provided—alas, in vain—for the constitution of a transition government and a united National Defense Committee to work in harmony until the declaration of independence. In Timor it was decided to hold a plebiscite to decide the political future of the colony, and Macao was no problem. China did not seem eager to integrate it (O Seculo, 1974a, 1974b) and demurred to clinch a friendly deal with a government much influenced by a pro-Soviet communist party.

VI. THE MARCH COUP

"Two clouds at least share the social horizon of Portugal at the beginning of 1975," wrote a Lisbon paper on New Year's Day. As far as the man in the street was concerned there was no doubt that the problems of political power and economic options were uppermost in everyone's mind. Both problems were closely linked.

The MFA was embarrassed by the coming elections, for a parliamentarian democracy precluded Third-World solutions—that is, military-revolutionary dictatorships—so much admired by fiery army militants. Prime Minister Vasco Gonçalves, the most precious pawn of the PCP in the very heart of the new ruling group, and Cunhal himself, were not interested in the establishment of a representative, parliamentarian democracy, and in this respect there was common ground between them and the radical-left, Maoist-Fidelist-Trotskyist-anarchist groups and grouplets.

The Intersindical decree had already been a step toward militarization of public life. With rare exceptions, such as *República,* the press and radio were already as tightly aligned with the left as they had been with the right under Caetano. But what the majority of the MFA refused to see was the boomerang effect of these measures. Intended to strengthen the MFA grip on the country, the measures had also strengthened the hand of the PCP. At the same time, however, they triggered a process of erosion of the new masters' credibility. Intersindical and *República* were the two Waterloos of the generals' popularity. They combined with a worsening of the economic situation. Another difficulty for the PCP-MDP team arose in the municipality and community councils where MDP mayors had occupied the city and town halls. At the end of February 1975, there was not the slightest doubt about the post-electoral fate of such local government institutions in the northern half of the country, where three-quarters of the Portuguese live: self-imposed mayors either would have to leave—or stay on in opposition to the population and face the consequences. This was another reason why the PCP-MDP did not want the elections.

Finally, there was the economic crisis. Production was down: the GNP had plummeted by 6 percent in a single year. The PCP-led Intersindical urged the workers to work more and earn less, but they remembered this slogan from Caetano's factory inspectors. Thus "the battle for production" the PCP tried to organize in the following months never came about. The permanent *saneamentos* (political purges) that left-wing radicals were conducting in the industrial sector robbed the country of civil engineers, shipbuilders, and technicians, who preferred emigration to Brazil to being submitted to perpetual inquisitorial inquiries about their "pro-Caetano past."

It is true that President Costa Gomes, a cautious and experienced patriot, tried to control the cataclysmic mood of the country. He had visited the United Nations in New York, and on October 18, 1974, accompanied by Foreign Minister Soares, conferred with President Ford and Secretary of State Kissinger. The result was the signing of an economic assistance agreement by which Portugal received over $75 million for housing, agriculture, transportation, education, and health programs (Cunhal, 1975: 171-172). But that was only a drop in the ocean. Portugal needed hundreds of millions of dollars that could only come from the European Economic Community. But the United States and the EEC, before extending further assistance, wanted proof that the money would not be used to back a left-wing dictatorship. The Portuguese press commented that the Western powers had not been so shy when the former regime had asked for financial help to back a right-wing dictatorship.

Communist Party initiatives only aggravated the situation in Portugal. The government, via the statements of one of the ministers, Dr. Rui Vilar, at the beginning of December 1974, affirmed its intent not to clip the wings of free enterprise. The pro-communist MDP thought that such a position indicated dangerous softness. Whereas government sources stressed that competition among middle-sized and small firms must be encouraged and not crippled—and whereas a special plan of antimonopolist legislation, favorable to middle-sized and small businesses had been prepared by a commission presided over by Dr. Vasco Airào of Oporto University—the MDP announced the arrest of "capitalists" and contractors on December 13, 1974. It was not surprising that citizen arrests by party vigilantes not only did not encourage middle-sized and small businessmen, but induced many of them to leave the country. In harmony with the MDP attacks on "monopolistic capital," Cunhal lashed out against "village capitalists": speaking at Alpiarça, he attacked the *Associação Livre dos Agricultores* (ALA), a professional body of well-off farmers, accusing it of links with persons who at that very moment were plotting against the revolution. Cunhal was not the only one warning of dark plots. Many press organs echoed rumors about an impending coup, and even the London *Economist* reported that "the toughest army units" were on the verge of rising against a regime that was plunging Portugal into an economic and political crisis.

Meanwhile, the former president of the Republic, General Spínola, was spending his time at his *Quinta das Flores* (The Flower Farm) at Massama, receiving many people who came to pay him a visit and apparently quite unaware that the COPCON intelligence kept a tight watch. The PCP weekly *Avante!* announced in every issue that a reactionary coup was impending, and Cunhal did the same in his public appearances. The gist of these utterances was that on the eve of grave events that endangered the revolution it might be more important to strengthen proletarian vigilance than to indulge in a preelectoral campaign. The coming elections clearly loomed as a headache for the party, and any dramatic event capable of postponing them promised to be an undisguised blessing.

The much-awaited coup took place on March 11, 1975. Having been so well anticipated, it was no surprise that it ended in dismal failure. Some old planes strafed the barracks of RAL, the Light Artillery Regiment, known for its penetration by PRP-BR agitators. Eight Alouette helicopters carried some 100 paratroopers from the Tancos Air Force base and landed at Sacavém, near the RAL barracks. Strangely enough, TV cameras were on the scene minutes after the landing, and they filmed the confrontation between the captain commanding the paratroopers, Sebastião Martins, and an artillery captain from the barracks, Diniş de Almeida. Almeida told Martins about the errors of his action, and Martins was soon convinced. At the same time four high-ranking Spinolist officers, led by General Damião, appeared at the National Guard barracks and had the pro-communist General Pinto Ferreira arrested. But when they heard about the outcome of the Sacavém affair and the failure of Spinolist mutineers to gain the control of Lisbon's airport, the officers fled to the German Embassy and asked for political asylum. General Carvalho had taken the supreme command of the battle against the rebellion and won it in several hours. The battle claimed one fatality—a soldier—and several injured. General Spínola and a handful of faithful officers fled to Spain in military helicopters piloted by rebel Air Force officers. The Portuguese Air Force commanding Sabre jet fighters did not try to prevent the Spinolists' flight.[34]

Once in exile, Spínola did not give an adequate explanation of the bizarre events. He alluded only to a plot to kill him, and criticized bitterly the "communist-dominated chaos for which the Caeteno regime had prepared Portugal." His fellow officers repeated the usual platitudes about their refusal to exchange one dictatorship for another.

The nagging question is how an experienced general and statesman like Spínola could have launched such an ill-advised venture. True, his experience in practical politics was limited. At the same time, it seems certain that he had given some credence to the rumor that the LUAR was planning a *matança da páscoa*, an "Easter Massacre" that would have liquidated from 1,000 to 1,500 rich bourgeois and dignitaries of the old regime, Spínola included. The draft of the speech the general intended to broadcast after his victory reveals the political line that he planned to adopt upon his return to power: he intended to explain that left-radical officers had perverted the original MFA program and that he, Spínola, came back to leadership in order to permit free Portugal to return to the pure wellsprings of the April coup. There was nothing in the draft about reprisals against the extreme-left enemies of the former president. The document bears out that Spínola entertained hopes of success. Given the insignificant number of military forces that took active part in the rebellion, the only conclusion to be drawn is that the Spinolists had expected the support of a considerable portion of the Portuguese armed forces. One theory depicts the whole affair as a consummate trap. According to this theory, Spínola, whose links with some possible schemes of rebellion were known to the COPCON, was approached by Air Force and other officers who not only promised him their backing but also urged the general to strike as soon as possible, the time having come for the restoration of law and order. Actually these officers were COPCON and PCP adherents with the mission of luring the hero of the moderates to his own ruin (Blackmann, 1975).[35] These gentlemen also fed Spínola with false intelligence about an impending "Easter Massacre" and about regiments ready to mutiny. In one afternoon the still-powerful Spinolist camp was finished off as a legal opinion movement. What lends credibility to this theory is that among Spínola's enemies there was a man like General Carvalho, former head of psychological warfare services in Portuguese Guinea, who had routinely dealt in devious stratagies for years, as well as the PCP leaders, heirs to a time-honored bag of tricks—a favorite one being to encourage the opposition to organize itself in order thereby to eliminate it more effectively (Hook, 1975: 62-63). If the theory holds, Spínola and his friends were victims of one of the most brilliant political hoaxes in contemporary history. Other circumstantial factors lending weight to the hoax theory included the lightning rapidity with which COPCON reacted, the swift reorganization of the whole structure of the top governing circle which took place within hours, and the loud praises lavished by Prime Minister Goncalves on the perspicacity of the PCP, which, according to him, alone of all political parties had rightly predicted what was going to happen.

The very same day of Spínola's misfired bid for power, a new top governmental institution was created: the Supreme Revolutionary Council (SRC), which included the members of the former Junta of National Salvation, the prime minister, the COPCON commander, the MFA Coordinating Committee, and other personalities. The Council's membership of 24 was expanded to 28 on March 22. The SRC assumed not only the right to veto decrees passed by the Cabinet, but also full legislative powers. The dramatics that surrounded the SRC's establishment, the mass demonstrations against "the forces of reaction," the solemn funeral of the lone soldier who had lost his life in the course of the *intentona* (attempted putsch), the "revolutionary" in the SRC's name—these all gave a new turn to the course of politics. The PCP, the extreme left-wingers, and even the PS spoke openly of the socialist revolution into which the democratic revolution was being transformed, but they involved different concepts of this revolution. The PCP exhorted the socialist revolution in oral propaganda, sticking to the democratic one in its publications. The PS let it be understood that the process would have nothing in common with the 1917 October Revolution, but might take instead the form of a legislative push that would transform the country into a kind of "Scandinavia in the sun," with heavy taxes on companies, excise duties on luxury articles, a progressive system of deductions in the taxation of the individual, a policy of levelling differences between individual incomes, a reduction in working hours, better housing conditions through land nationalization and state initiative—and all this crowned by a string of welfare services.

Such "pragmatic" programs, however, provoked only contempt from the left-radical ranks. They wanted a socialist revolution faithful to the classical model—bloody and romantic, with violence wreaked against the bourgeoisie and imperialist agents. Proof of the radicalization of both the MFA general assembly and of the MFA men in the SRC could be seen in the rise of César Oliveira, a MES leader, who was gaining so much influence that he was jokingly referred to as "the 29th member of the SRC." Oliveira stressed always that the *saneamento* (political purge) had been carried out feebly and that it must be conducted with more thoroughness.[36] Oliveira's rise must be understood also in the context of the desire of MFA leaders to obtain the services of a Marxist counsellor who was independent of the PCP and headed a political group too small to give offense.

In any event, the constitutional changes did not stop with the enthroning of the SRC. On March 13, the civilian members of the Council of State, an institution shaded by the new developments, presented their resignation; it was another step on the way to the militarization of public life. This aim was consummated on April 2, when the political parties were asked to sign "a platform of agreement" that represented in effect the draft of a new constitution even before the elections to the Constituent Assembly. The MFA obtained from the principal political parties their assent to the military governing the country for another period of three to five years, irrespective of the results of the coming elections. The MFA also insisted that whatever the new constitution to be shaped by the future constituent assembly, its main provisions must state that the president of the Republic would always be the same person as the commander-in-chief of the armed forces, and that he should be given the right to dissolve any future legislative assembly upon consultation with the Cabinet and the Council of State.[37] The MFA thus imposed a general as head of state "for all eternity."

The man who conducted the negotiations with the political parties was not President Costa Gomes, but Prime Minister Gonçalves, who less than ten days before, on March 23, had formed a new provisional government. His new team represented another step in the process of militarization and radicalization. The foreign affairs post was taken from Dr. Soares and given to a MFA leader, Major Antunes; Dr. Soares stayed on in the Cabinet as Minister without Portfolio. The government included eight officers and only seven civilians. Among the latter, João Cardona Gomes Cravinho, Minister for Industry and Technology, represented by his connection with MES the first discreet entry of left-wing radicalism into a Portuguese government. President Costa Gomes tried to assuage the misgivings of the democratic parties at their lack of representation with the explanation that it was necessary for the MFA to impose a somewhat "controversial" platform of agreement, given the political ignorance of the Portuguese nation. The new scheme of things, stressed Costa Gomes, was vital against "autocratic, reactionary, or pseudo-revolutionary parties."

The crisis triggered by the abortive Spinolist coup brought the relations between the PCP and the PS to new boiling points—the origins of which, however, antedated the events of March 11. As was noted above, Cunhal had articulated forebodings about an impending Spinolist coup, and he exploited this to put the PS into a difficult position. At a party meeting on September 9, Cunhal addressed himself solemnly to the PS leadership, asking Soares, in view of the terrible dangers ready to pounce on the country, to stop electoral polemics. The communist leader summoned his socialist colleague to cease on the spot all criticism of the PCP and to join him within the framework of a "Unity of Action Agreement." Soares replied that he could accept the proposal if the PCP took the engagement to assent to "a pluralistic democracy" and to "socialism in liberty." Cunhal did not assent. Immediately after Spinola's misadventure, Cunhal accused Soares and the socialist leadership of having been Spinola's accomplices. He invoked as proof of this allegation that an officer seen with Spinola had also been seen some four months before at the PS convention. It was therefore "a crime by association." Cunhal's polemics signalled into the streets thousands of demonstrators demanding a revolutionary tribunal to mete out justice to the plotters against "the people." Carvalho's COPCON, which had arrested a group of rich businessmen (Jorge de Melo and some members of the Espírito Santo dynasty among them) sent its armed brigades to guard PS and PPD headquarters, beseiged by crowds of left-wing radicals. Incidentally, Carvalho nearly provoked a diplomatic incident when he implied that U.S. Ambassador Frank C. Carlucci had perhaps been involved in Spinola's plot. After several days of reflection, the COPCON commander withdrew his statement. General Carvalho had also let armed workers' groups and enthusiastic left-wingers go down to the beaches to fight against a possible attack by the U.S. Navy, but the Americans disappointed by not invading Portugal.[38]

The Spinola debacle strengthened the PCP, but it strengthened the MFA far more. The PCP did not accomplish its priority objective: the indefinite postponement of the elections. On this point President Costa Gomes and a majority group in the MFA leadership stood firm. Both the communists and the ruling officers knew what the PCP could expect from these elections—even if they underestimated the PCP defeat. Nevertheless, the Spínola catastrophe bestowed its blessings on the communists; their faithful Gonçalves headed the new government. The leader of the MDP, Professor Pereira de Moura, was back in the Cabinet, and the Ministry of Transportation was given to a communist. The Minister for the Interior, Major Metelo, could be considered a Gonçalves man, and the important Ministry of Economic Planning fell to Murteira, again an MDP man. The communists played down the nomination of Industry Minister Cravinho, considered a representative of radical left-wing (MES) influence in the Cabinet, by suggesting that he was an MDP man. The PCP could consider even the dismissal of Dr. Soares as Foreign Minister and his replacement by Major Melo Antunes as a communist victory.

Nevertheless, the MFA leaders were the real winners of the coup and its aftermath. They achieved what they called the "institutionalization" of their movement, and reached two of their immediate goals:

(1) the part of the Portuguese army that had not taken part in the revolutionary movement against Caetano—that is by far the majority of the officers—could now be put to make the choice: to accept MFA hegemony over the whole of the armed forces, or to be purged as "Spínolists," and

(2) a sort of "state within the state," could now be established, purely military in character, and forming the frame of a "soldiers and officers" society, complete with military Cabinet (the SRC), military parliament (the MFA General Assembly), and local institutions (the military regions assemblies).

Elated as they were with their victory over Spínola, the MFA leading men had, however, maneuvered themselves into a position fraught with danger: their "state within the state" was in fact a military society living at the expense of civil society. Because of the very nature of the composition (particularly the absence of any women), the MFA was completely out of touch with daily economic problems, prices, marketing, and production. Functioning on a wage that was regularly and rather generously adjusted to rising prices, the members of the MFA assemblies could indulge in the most utopian projects. There were other dangers: the grass roots and general assemblies of the MFA could paralyze the SRC just as democratic parliaments can paralyze cabinets. Nobody could prevent PCP or left-wing radical officers from manipulating barracks elections. A situation was created where a handful of soldiers, sergeants, and junior officers, painfully lacking political or cultural sophistication, could dictate to the high-ranking officers of the SRC, who lived with the apprehension of not being considered revolutionary enough. In order to survive politically, the new MFA establishment was condemned to ignore the aspirations of civilian society.

The Spínola discomfiture had its consequences in the economic field as well: in order to punish the rich people who were supposed to have financed the general's attempt, or at least hoped to profit by his restoration, the SRC issued decrees nationalizing insurance companies and privately owned banks, with the exception of foreign banks branches. The nationalization idea was suggested by "councils of bank employees" dominated by the PCP leadership and the left-wing radicals, but it seemed to take the PCP leadership somewhat by surprise. Premier Goncalves, announcing these measures and presenting them as an instance of "antimonopolistic policy," hinted at the "antimonopolistic strategy" promised by the first MFA manifesto. President Costa Gomes defined the nationalization as "the most revolutionary decree issued in this country." It was the end of the "20 families" who had owned the Portuguese economy under the cozy reigns of Salazar and Caetano, but nobody knew of what it was the beginning.

VII. THE VOICE OF THE PEOPLE

An American weekly wrote, after the failure of the Spínolist coup, that if Spínola himself ever got his deserts, the monocled ex-general (he has been dishonorably discharged from the Portuguese army) might logically be considered a candidate for the Order of Lenin. This award is not for the Portuguese to give. Yet, it is true that the myopia manifested by the plotters, and more generally the lack of perspicacity shown by the top businessmen of the country, encouraged the MFA stalwarts in thinking that half a century of Salazarism had brought about a profound degeneration of the upper bourgeoisie's power of will and clearness of judgment. If Portuguese capitalism were a giant with feet of clay, its overthrow would be an easy and popular task. The government had ready a decree allowing it to nationalize all firms managed "unsatisfactorily." The wording was vague, ominous, and obviously intended to frighten the middle class.

These muted threats proved to be premature. The ruling group deemed that the time was not yet ripe for further nationalization. The state of economy was precarious. The last political purges and the intimidations to which technicians, professional men, and skilled craftsmen suspected of Spinolism were subjected had driven from the country hundreds of these needed talents. Unemployment was rising steadily, and thousands of destitute refugees from Mozambique and Angola were landing on Portugal's shores. Later on, MFA leaders would try to woo industrialists (those who had not left), and to explain to them that private property still had a role to play in an economy shifting to socialism (Expresso, 1975g).

The MFA leaders, with their PCP-MDP allies, presented the impending elections as the opportunity for the people to choose the road to socialism against those who stood for the continuing dominance of monopolistic capitalism. But between the Spínola coup on March 11 and Election Day on April 25 enough happened to help the two biggest political parties of the country, the PS and the PPD, remind the electorate that the option "a people's Portugal versus monopolistic sharks" was not at all the real issue. For the PS, the issue was "a free, democratic, pluralistic socialism versus totalitarianism and dictatorship"; for the PPD, it was "pluralistic democracy versus authoritarian regime." As the huge majority of the Portuguese were working people, it was not a regime of greater social justice that they feared. Having just emerged from half a century of dictatorship, they were weary of the banning of political parties, of party monopoly, of the media, of arrests made without a judge's writ, of censorship, of local and regional authorities imposed from above, of small minorities dictating the behavior of the majority, and of a government fearful of freedom.

Immediately after the Spinola putsch, the Gonçalves Cabinet hurried to ban the PDC, the Christian Democratic Party led by Major Sanches Osório, a Spinola man. But the government also banned left-wing groups: the ADC, the "Alliance of Workers and Farm Laborers," and the MRPP, the most militant of Maoist groups. Characteristically, the MRPP was banned on March 28 because it refused to delete the hammer and sickle from its banners. These leftist groups were prevented from taking an active part in public life because they had criticized the PCP leaders. A banning of left-wing groups could not be justified in terms of the fight against "monopolistic sharks." Both the PS and the PPD pointed out that these measures expressed the will of the PCP leaders not to tolerate free speech and open criticism and that the actions had absolutely nothing to do with economic or social issues.

With respect to the press, the situation was bad enough with the main papers under firm PCP-MDP control. After Spinola's downfall the Gonçalves people found a man fitted for the post of State Secretary of Information: this happened to be the director of the principal Lisbon prison, Lieutenant-Colonel Conçeicao e Silva. Portugal's journalists thought it ominous to see the liberty of the press in the custody of a man fresh from such a job (Le Monde, 1974a). Meanwhile, the new Minister of Social Communication, Major Jorge Correia Jesuino, utilized the time until the elections to make some disastrous (for the extreme radical MFA officers) comments on the current situation. On April 3 he explained that popular consultation by means of general elections would not determine who should lead the nation: "We [MFA leaders] are the vanguard of that revolution and thus have the right to assume the direction of the nation." On April 10, he even regretted publicly that freedom had been given by the MFA to political parties. As Major Jesuino saw it, the free thrashing out of public issues—political activity as understood in the West—had "hampered" the work of the MFA. Having thus criticized unmentioned parties, but meaning quite obviously the PS and the PPD, Jesuino wound up by praising the PCP for its "efficacy" (Le Monde, 1974e).

Major Jesuino's remarks probably did not profit the parties backed by the left wing of the MFA. The PCP and its MDP appendix (the left-radical groups taking part in the elections) were not seen as having any chance at the polls, yet the remarks were but another indication that MFA headquarters was insensitive to the mood of the country. Ten days before the elections the ruling officers, who had advised undecided voters to cast blank ballots, thought that in such a way it would be clearly demonstrated that the "toiling masses" were as yet not ripe for pluralistic party democracy and needed the MFA as a tutor. Jesuino joined his comrades in anticipating that 70 percent of the ballots would turn up blank (Le Monde, 1974d); whereas the actual number turned out to be 7 percent.

The PCP, whatever the private misgivings of its Central Committee, seemed cocksure of a splendid showing at the elections, or at least tried to give that impression. At a huge meeting in Lisbon on March 18, Cunhal listened to his supporters chanting, "There is only one solution: to shoot the reaction!"—a statement to which he voiced his opposition. Yet, the faithful were prepared for dismal results. Around March 23 they knew already that if the PS and PPD should win the elections proof would be invoked that the elections had not been democratic (Le Monde, 1974c, 1974f).[39] The PCP made a tremendous effort to conquer the yet-undecided, but unofficially its leading members admitted that their party would not get more than 20 percent of the vote (it received 12 percent). The communists probably spent more money on posters, placards, propaganda bills, and brochures than all the other parties combined. Wonderfully organized, commanding electoral squadrons that broke up the rallies of "reactionary parties," the PCP's influence, mainly physical, forced the PPD leaders to barricade themselves in their Lisbon headquarters, and frightened many citizens into thinking they would risk their safety by voting freely. Incidentally, this behavior was not looked upon indifferently by Carvalho's COPCON, which did not like to see its own monopoly of public power challenged by political parties.

The PS approached the elections with growing confidence. In the southern half of the country rival vigilantes hampered the socialist electoral canvassing, but at the last elections in the trade union the PCP was retreating in the face of a socialist upsurge. The *freguesias* committees, local authorities, mayors, and district governors manned by MDP activists and other PCP front personalities, were treated with progressive unkindness by the population at large. The PS also received a surprising gift from the MFA several days before April 25, the first anniversary of the 1974 coup that had been chosen as election day. Whereas Cunhal and his comrades were attacking Dr. Soares as a pro-Spinolist plotter in every speech, the MFA published the findings of the commission of inquiry charged to bring to light the truth about the Spinola coup attempt. Even if the whole truth was not yet revealed, the commission did at least find that there were in the Spinolist camp people who planned to assassinate both Soares and the socialist Minister of Justice, Salgado Zenha. To the socialist's astonishment, the PCP speakers went on talking about Soares' part in the plot, as if no findings had been published, but public opinion was favorably impressed both by the

TABLE 2

Name of district	% of voters .	ballot-papers	CDS	MDP	MES	PCP	PPD	PPM	PSP	UDP
AVEIRO	91.79%	5.26	11.6	3.89	0.99	3.01	42.94	---	31.73	---
BEJA	91.77	7.43	2.19	5.46	2.53	39.01	5.23	---	35.49	1.43
BRAGA	93.00	6.37	18.06	2.92	0.81	3.69	37.70	0.75	27.44	---
BRAGANÇA	90.82	9.92	13.51	3.64	---	2.70	43.08	1.02	24.55	---
CASRELO BRANCO	90.67	11.29	6.40	3.97	2.18	5.65	24.35	0.75	41.31	0.73
COIMBRA	89.12	10.01	4.68	4.46	1.67	5.72	27.15	0.93	43.28	---
ÉVORA	94.26	4.82	2.82	7.89	---	37.14	6.84	---	37.76	0.85
FARO	90.65	9.18	3.35	9.49	1.59	12.30	18.91	---	45.45	1.12
GUARDA	91.92	9.85	19.49	3.58	---	2.93	33.39	1.89	28.16	---
LEIRIA	89.81	10.12	6.76	3.37	1.11	6.44	35.55	---	33.15	1.07
LISBON	91.95	5.71	4.79	4.11	1.08	18.95	14.91	0.72	46.05	1.67
PORTALEGRE	94.44	7.30	3.97	4.54	1.28	17.53	9.82	0.58	52.40	1.20
OPORTO	93.84	5.25	3.94	2.57	0.99	6.65	29.42	0.56	42.48	0.63
SANTARÉM	91.67	8.67	4.33	4.08	1.56	15.10	18.79	1.16	42.89	1.03
SETÚBAL	93.27	5.49	1.55	6.03	1.02	37.82	5.74	---	38.15	1.34
VIANA DO CASTELO	88.63	8.81	14.54	7.06	1.54	3.80	36.01	1.10	24.36	---
VILA REAL	89.29	11.39	7.08	2.31	---	2.56	46.00	1.08	27.00	---
VISEU	89.22	8.00	17.26	4.04	---	2.27	43.89	0.91	21.33	---

AZORES ISLANDS

Name of district	% of voters .	ballot-papers	CDS	MDP	MES	PCP	PPD	PPM	PSP	UDP
ANGRA	90.39	3.55	6.10	1.03	1.19	2.25	62.84	---	22.90	---
HORTA	89.77	4.06	---	3.11	---	2.33	67.60	---	22.91	---
PONTA DELSADA	90.46	6.85	3.09	2.70	0.72	1.47	54.83	---	30.34	---

MADEIRA

Name of district	% of voters .	ballot-papers	CDS	MDP	MES	PCP	PPD	PPM	PSP	UDP
FUNCHAL	89.10	4.43	10.03	1.29	---	1.63	62.05	---	19.43	---

CDS (CENTRO DEMOCRATICO SOCIAL) right-of-center party.
MDP (MOVIMENTO DEMOCRATICO PORTUGUES) a communist-front organization.
MES (MOVIMENTO DA ESNUERDA SOCIALISTA) radical, non-Leninist, left-wing party.
PCP (PARTIDO COMUNISTA PORTUGUES) the communist party.
PPD (PARTIDO POPULAR DEMOCRATICO) a left-of-center (social-democratic) party.
PPM (PARTIDO POPULAR MONARQUICO) a royalist party.
PSP (PARTIDO SOCIALISTA PORTUGUES) the socialist party.
UDP (UNIAO DEMOCRATICA POPULAR) radical left-wing party, anti-PCP.

honesty of the commission of inquiry and by the evidence of a certain fear in a part of the ruling military circles of too-strong a showing by the PCP; the timing of the release of the findings could hardly have been explained otherwise. On the eve of the elections, President Costa Gomes addressed himself to the nation by radio and television appealing to the citizens to exercise their rights—a veiled criticism of the "blank ballot" advice given by extremist MFA officers—to embrace party pluralism, to reject extremist tendencies and to vote in favor of socialism.

There was a very heavy turnout in the elections: 92 percent of those qualified voted. The people of Portugal, going to polling stations in their Sunday finery, manifested by the joy and calm they displayed how highly they valued the first free elections in their country after half a century (the last having been held in November 1925).

The PS polled 37.87 percent of the total vote; the PPD 26.38 percent; the PCP 12.53 percent; the CDS 7.65 percent; the MPD 4.12 percent; MES 1.02 percent; PPM 0.56 percent; the UDP 0.79 percent; and FSP, a left-wing splinter group 1.17 percent. Other unimportant left-wing lists drew respectively 0.57 percent; 0.19 percent; and 0.23 percent (Portugal Socialista, 1975a). Thus the votes of 5,665,707 Portuguese men and women resulted in the election of a Constituent Assembly comprehending five main political groups and respresented by the following numbers of deputies: PS –115; PPD –80; PCP –30; CDS –16; MDP –5; UDP –1; Macau Local List –1; PS of Mozambique –1. In fact, the political groups were only four, as the MDP identified itself with the PCP. Some features of these elections came as a surprise to the Portuguese themselves. The elections had been quite free, the army and the COPCON preventing trouble-makers from disturbing the polling. The "blank ballots" scheme of the MFA left wing proved a total failure; the refusal of the electorate to follow advice aimed at showing the political idiocy of the "toiling masses" strengthened the socialist and social-democratic claims to a "pluralistic" democracy based on political parties.

The electoral results drew a new political map of the country: whereas the south showed the greatest concentration of PCP votes, and the north turned to be a stronghold of the PPD, the PS appeared as more or less equally spread in strength over the whole of Portugal, emerging actually as the one real national party. It had obtained astonishingly good results in regions and cities considered as bases of PCP power: undoubtedly a reaction of working class voters to the methods used by the PCP in trade union matters led them to vote for the PS. The PPD, the second-largest political party, proved by its success (generally in regions where the right-of-center CDS was considered the main political force) that social democracy was more appreciated by the urban and rural lower-middle classes than conservatism. Incidentally, the PPD's good showing and the CDS' weak one proved inane the claims of PCP-MDP controlled papers concerning the sway of reactionary extreme-conservative elements on all of northern Portugal.

The PPD had profited from the fact that 18 of the 21 cities with a population above 10,000 were situated in the north of the country, and received the title of "the party of the small cities"—an important advantage in Portugal where there are only two large cities.

The elections had two immediate effects. Cunhal, at the head of the PCP, followed by the MDP, delivered a statement to the effect that elections are, after all, of no importance whatsoever. The entire PCP-MDP-controlled press, radio, and television network followed suit in explaining that democracy does *not* mean free elections, parliamentarian representation, or basic freedoms; rather, according to these people, democracy is the people's power—the people's most conscious part being the proletariat, the vanguard of which is the communist party led by its secretary general. The extreme left of the MFA sincerely played down the elections. Prime Minister Gonçalves hastened to explain that the electoral results would not change the composition of the government, which decided to ignore them completely. Major Jesuino stated that one year is not enough to allow millions of citizens to acquire political consciousness, suggesting that the present elections only had the merit of proving that sad fact. The initial effect of the elections was thus one of deepening the chasm between the *pais real*—actual Portugal—and the one perceived by the military-political power elite.

The second effect was the tremendous political awakening of the Portuguese people during and after the election campaign, albeit not in the sense desired by the majority of its rulers. Portugal remembered that Salazar had not only been against socialism and communism, but even more against democracy and parliamentarianism—that, indeed, Salazar had claimed that the democratic-parliamentary system must be annihilated because it would finally bring socialism upon the country. In April 1975 the nation recognized, in its depths, that only the respect of the people's will, as demonstrated in the electoral results, can prevent a new dictatorship.

The fear that a part of the MFA could be lured away from the intimacy with the PCP in which Premier Gonçalves thought his comrades must learn to live induced the communist leadership to attempt a limited show of force. First it obtained from the SRC a solemn recognition that the PCP-dominated trade union central, the *Intersindical,* was indeed the sole legal trade union confederation. This was a May Day 1975 present from the MFA to Cunhal and his comrades intended to soothe the irritations caused in the party's ranks by the poor electoral showing and to proclaim outwardly that the mutual confidence between MFA and PCP remained as strong as ever. Thereupon, the ushers at the May Day meeting of the Intersindical prevented the PS Secretary-General, Dr. Soares, from entering the stadium where the official meeting was in progress. As the PPD, which included thousands of workers in its ranks, had not been even invited at all to the meeting, and with the socialists symbolically turned away, it appeared that Gonçalves, Cunhal, and their friends considered only those 16.65 percent of the Portuguese who had voted for the PCP-MDP lists as worthy to be numbered among the workers permitted to rejoice on May Day (Sousa, 1975a).

In light of these incidents, which substantiated the impossibility of collaboration between the two worker's parties, some of the MFA leaders began to play anew with their pet idea: namely, the creation of MFA's own political organization. In theory, normal relations between PS and PCP leaders could have achieved a sort of civilian "popular front" that would finally have sent the generals back to their barracks. But this was an idea in theory only. Cunhal and his men preferred to work directly with the officers, the possibility of using the chains of command and the professional discipline of the military being far more alluring than perpetual negotiations with another party leadership, with which power would have to be divided. The Vice-Admiral Antonio Rosa Coutinho, a SRC member who had been one of the initiators of the "blank ballot" movement again began to agitate for his "civilian MFA" plan (Sousa, 1975b). He spoke of "rainbow-color socialism"—not PCP-color—and stressed that only by establishing such a mass movement would the MFA leaders be freed from their dependence on political parties. Central figures in the MFA reacted favorably to this possible way of delivering them from the need of collaborating with the parties (with the exceptions of Vasco Gonçalves and half dozen close political friends in the SRC, who were quite willing to collaborate at least with one party—the PCP).

The mass meeting on May 2 in Lisbon that was called by the Socialist Party to protest the actions of the authorities at the May Day meeting the day before and that was held despite official prohibition had demonstrated that the PS would not yield its role as the largest political party of the country. It also served as a new reminder to the MFA that pluralistic party democracy is a cumberstone affair. Gonçlaves' expectation that the PCP would emerge strong and large enough to be the one party upon which the MFA could base its policies had been aborted: the PCP had not succeeded in obtaining a clear-cut victory even in the industrial areas in which it represented itself as the dominant political force. At Beja, the main communist stronghold, the PS emerged nearly equal in strength in Setúbal city and district, a region of historical communist predominance in working neighborhoods; the PCP and PS sent to the assembly the same number of deputies. Even more distressing for Goncalves' theory was the lack of any real prospects of future improvements in the PCP's position: as the single well-organized Portuguese party, the PCP had strained its strength to the utmost—as such the meager results that it gleaned in the elections were obviously the maximum it could obtain. By contrast, the two other young and bigger parties, PS and PPD, stood only at the beginning of their organizational drives, and could look to further inroads into the demoralized CDS on the right and the beaten MDP on the left.

If the MFA wanted to rule in relative tranquility, it would have to scrap the party system altogether. The PCP, for reasons already mentioned, was also eager to have the party system abolished—that is, with the vital exception of itself and its appendix, the MDP. If, until the eve of the elections, Cunhal and his paper,

Avante!, attacked the "brotherly" socialist party for its alleged weaknesses towards Spinola, after the elections the PCP started to characterize the PS as a "reactionary force." In any case, for the PCP, the pro-PCP wing of the MFA, and the radical-left camp the Election Day of April 25 was Black Friday. In order to erase it from the peoples' minds, the revolutionary process had to be speeded up with utmost energy.

This acceleration took various forms. The PS and PPD could be "democratically" displaced only if another kind of political pattern would emerge in their stead. In this spirit, Vice-Admiral Rosa Coutinho had proposed a "civilian MFA." The PCP, for its part, pressed for the establishment of "Committees for the Defense of the Revolution" in every neighborhood, every factory, and every regiment. The radical left-wingers had begun even before Black Friday to organize "revolutionary councils" that were brought together in a national convention in Lisbon on April 19-20; their purpose was to stress the importance of combining workers and soldiers in the same councils, thus sapping the prestige of the MFA leadership in the barracks and undermining the authority of the PCP and its Intersindical in the industrial sector (Sousa, 1975c).

The most spectacular "speeding-up" measure, however, was the closing of the pro-socialist evening daily *República*. This took place on the morning of the stormy May Day meeting in Lisbon—and it was done in a most sophisticated way. Workers in the paper's printing shop, who officially were *not* members of the PCP, felt too affronted by articles criticizing the PCP to print them. So they simply occupied the premises and evicted the pro-socialist editorial board. The Press Council, summoned by an alarmed PS invoking the guarantees concerning freedom of the press given by the MFA, decided in favor of the pro-socialist editorial board, while the PS leaders alternately appealed to President Costa Gomes and threatened to bring the case before a tribunal. The Gonçalves Cabinet, after muddling through lengthy ratiocinations, agreed with the Press Council. But when it came to hand over the *República* premises to its legal owners, General Carvalho's COPCON acted in the spirit of proletarian solidarity and strengthened the workers' hold on the illegally occupied property. It was the *República* affair that rendered the regime in Lisbon the worst service possible by focusing world attention on the Portuguese situation and eliciting unfavorable comments from circles generally well-disposed toward the Portuguese revolution, including even the Italian communists (Corriere della Sera, 1975c).

Another "speeding up" phenomenon occurred when the discreet "gentlemen's agreement" between the new regime and the Portuguese Church broke down into a violent conflict. The Church had always been a citadel of conservatism in Portugal, and nothing resembling phenomena like the French "priest workers" *(prêtres ouvriers)* or the left-wing Spanish curates could be discerned in its ranks until the last days of Caetano's regime. During Salazar's reign in July 1958, the Bishop of Oporto, Antonio Ferreira Gomes, had dared to send a more-or-less open letter to the dictator in which the Bishop warned that the attempt to identify the Church with the Estado Novo would result in great misfortunes for the Church, the weakening of religion, and the self-compromise of the Catholic hierarchy. For his frankness, Bishop Gomes was exiled and had to spend ten years abroad.

Yet, the Portuguese Church indeed identified itself with the dictatorship and blessed the soldiers departing for the colonial wars. The number of dissenters in the Church was insignificant. After the April 1974 coup, following some years of malaise in Vatican-Portuguese relations because of the growing concern of the Papacy for the ultimate fate of Catholics in Portuguese Africa, the Cardinal-Patriarch of Lisbon, Antonio Ribeiro, head of the Portuguese Church, decided to collaborate with the new regime. But the Catholic hierarchy was compromised in the eyes of many believing Portuguese and bitterly criticized by newly organized lay groups such as the Guarda CERP ("Christians in Permanent Reflection") and the Oporto GRAI ("Group for Reflection, Action, and Intervention"). The PS drew the open support of many church-going Catholics, and a monk, Brother Bento Domingues (1975), advanced theological reasons for being a socialist.

Generally, the prophecy made by Bishop Gomes in his famous letter had been realized, and the Church could not easily dispel memories of its role under the dictatorship. Yet, the Catholic hierarchy was rescued from its predicament by an action that preceded the closing of *República* but seemed inspired by the same revolutionary tactics. The workers and technicians of the radio station *Renascença,* which belonged to the Portuguese episcopate, occupied the station and stopped its special programs—not because, as in the *República* case, the workers felt indignation at articles sent to the printers, but because this time they felt indignation about some reporting that was *not* broadcast. The frustrated Catholic listeners tuned in to "Radio Vatican," a Portuguese program that did nothing to calm the feelings of offended righteousness by the faithful. The bishops tried in vain to get their property back. The SRC and the government preferred to beat about the bush. It was a fatal mistake. The official procrastination incited Lisbon's Catholics to demonstrate their support to the episcopate on June 19, surrounded by thousands of radical left-wingers. The Catholic demonstrators were forced to seek refuge in the palace of the Cardinal-Archbishop of Lisbon, and had to be evacuated by the COPCON. In church-going northern Portugal these developments were deeply resented. Sporadic gun battles broke out between outraged Catholics and people they suspected of intending to curtail the liberties of the Church. Thus, without really trying, the MFA regime succeeded in getting itself involved in a Holy War. The Catholic hierarchy, which during the first weeks after the April coup had been busily trying to blot out the stigmas of its past support of dictatorship and colonialism, suddenly was transformed into a kind of public prosecutor—and a robbed prosecutor at that. The clumsiness of Vasco Gonçalves' dealings in the *Renascença* conflict helped to alienate the northern half of the country (which by dint of its population could better be described as the northern two thirds) even more from the new regime.

VIII. THE JULY 1975 CRISIS

The repeated refusal by the Vasco Gonçalves group in the regime to return *República* to its editorial board, to find a dignified compromise in the *Radio Renascença* affair, to allow free trade union elections, and to permit the victors in the general elections to replace the despised MDP governors, mayors, and municipal councils, heralded the crisis of July 1975. These events furnished incontrovertible proof that General Gonçalves was unable to steer a political course independent of the PCP.

The PCP press continued to ignore the election results, pretending that Cunhal and his comrades were great favorites with the masses and were disliked only by reactionaries. Inasmuch as these "reactionaries" numbered at least 83 percent of the Portuguese people, the pretensions of the PCP took on an air of tragicomedy. In an interview with Italian journalist Oriana Fallaci (1975), Cunhal said a number of things that illuminated communist tactics during the summer of 1975. For example, he stressed that the rules of the election game ought not to be accepted by him, and that Portugal would never be a country of democratic freedoms. Cunhal subsequently denied these assertions, but Signora Fallaci had taped the conversation.

Disquieting rumors about the fate of PIDE files, supposedly used to support a new secret police, added to the general nervousness. Probably as many as 20,000 individuals had at one time or another been in the service of the PIDE as secret agents; a group exploiting the files could thus blackmail its way to power. The PCP denied that its members had anything to do with the "refiling of the files," the "PIDE Liquidation Commission" having been a purely military institution. But on July 12, *Expresso* (1975e) published a deposition by one of the commission members, Fernando Oneto, who gave the names of five PCP members who had enjoyed access to the precious files.

Another cause for worry was the undisciplined behavior of some army units that decided to vent revolutionary fervor of their own. The "Red Regiment," 1st Light Artillery (RAL 1) was one such unit. On May 15, RAL soldiers arrested on their own initiative a sailor presumed to be an ELP agent—ELP being the illegal, right-wing "Army for the Liberation of Portugal." The sailor was delivered for interrogation to the Maoist group, MRPP, and the MRPP subsequently ordered its soldier friends to arrest a COPCON officer. The COPCON had to interfere. Such incidents were frequent. The penetration of military units by groups such as the MRPP put in danger the military discipline upon which MFA's pretentions to rule the country were based. The chief of the General Staff, General Fabião, complained about this state of things. Yet, there was nothing he could do as long as the April 25 elections were not respected. Lacking any base for political rule beyond the agreement it entered upon with the political parties, and respecting that agreement in a declining measure every day, the MFA stayed in power only by the force of its tanks. Such a shaky legal base invited violence by other forces in the country, such as the MRPP.

The RAL commander, for his part, liked to take his regiment out, in full battle array, to demonstrate against the legally and democratically elected Constituent Assembly. The commander, Dinis de Almeida, did not shy away from the prospect of a civil war. He placidly told the MFA General Assembly that on April 25, 1974, Portugal was fecundated by the MFA; on September 28, when Spinola was thrown out, the country felt the nausea of a pregnant woman; and in July 1975, the day of delivery was near. Almeida reminded his listeners that there is no bloodless childbirth (Corriere della Sera, 1975b).

The childbirth Almeida referred to obviously meant the coming revolution. On June 15, General Carvalho, the COPCON's commanders, gave an interview to *Rádio Renascença,* stressing that the Portuguese people were not yet aware of the terrible sacrifices required for a true revolution; in this respect, regretted the general, the Portuguese were far behind the Vietnamese and would do better to emulate the PAIGC in Guinea-Bissau, which shot scores of counter-revolutionaries immediately after taking power.

All these statements were directly inspired by Cunhal's thesis on "electoralism"—the term that he applied to representative democracy, Western style. "Electoralism," the respect of free elections, could only postpone or prevent the need for a revolution and meant eternal capitalism (a view, incidentally, that Italian or Spanish communists do not officially share). In any case, with "electoralism" Portugal would soon cease to be governed by the MFA, and would never be a PCP-ruled country—an intolerable thought for the MFA-PCP alliance.

All of these statements underscore the assumption that the July crisis must be considered only as the prolegomenon to the use of "revolutionary violence." Such violence will break out at a propitious moment for the users—that is, when an army faction ready to sustain such a "dictatorship of the proletariat" crystallizes with sufficient political clearness and sufficient fire power. The tactics of the SP, and in a lesser measure those of the PPD, were directed during the month of July toward preventing such a crystallization through a massive display of popular support destined to convince the would-be dictators and their praetorian guards that a new coup would be resisted.

On June 21, 1975, the MFA officers, aware of their dwindling popularity, published "Political Action Plan," which was possibly inspired by their MES counsellors. This vaguely worded plan promised to respect "political pluralism," but only if the "options" chosen by the political parties enjoying "pluralism" are in favor of constructing socialism. There were also hints of "popular organisms"—that is, local and factory councils that would serve as channels of basic democracy and consolidate the MFA-*Povo* union. Everybody took from the Political Action Plan what he liked: Dr. Soares was glad to find "pluralism" mentioned, and General Garvalho hinted that it would be better to stop the "sterile play" of party politics. But these measures were not "popular" enough to satisfy the MES or General Carvalho's favorite left-wing group, the PRP-BR. The PCP, for its part, pressed for the establishment of "Committees for the Defense of the Revolution" wherever possible.

All these supporters of "basic forms of democracy"—the MFA, PCP, and left-radical groups—shared the priority objective of stopping the ascendancy of the PS. Dr. Soares' party enjoyed growing popularity, as the main antitotalitarian force in the country. A foreign observer of the Portuguese scene, the French political writer Gilles Martinet (1975), estimated that if free elections were held in the summer of 1975, the PS would have achieved absolute majority throughout Portugal.

The MFA leadership's answer was a new plan published on July 9. The avowed aim of the plan was the establishment of "the people's power." It meant that nonpartisan "basic assemblies" of inhabitants would manage their local affairs and, in a way not clearly explained, rule the socialist Portugal that they would help to build. An indication of what the planners had in mind came with the publication on July 12 of a sample project for a "local people's power organization." This document has special significance because the initiators of the "sample project" were the same ones who presented the whole social reconstruction plan to the MFA General Assembly and had it adopted: the soldiers and officers of the First Engineers Regiment of Pontinha-Lisbon.

The scope of the "sample project" included six suburbs of the capital: Campo Grande, Benfica, São Domingos, Carnide, Carnaxide, and Odivelas. The project, drafted in the style of a military attack order, starts with the description of the goal to be attained and continues with the analysis of the social forces engaged in the operation, their functioning, and hierarchy. According to the project, the new forms of popular state power must erase individualism and selfishness, and must create a collective conscience and a true popular culture. As a way toward such lofty aims "secret votes are prohibited, all decisions having to be taken by raising the arm *(braço no ar)* in an open vote." Liberty of expression and discussion is permitted in questions of general interest; but there is no mechanism to determine what is considered of general interest. Finally, the individual who misbehaves at the local people's power assembly or boycotts it, refusing even to engage in self-criticism, will be punished (Expresso, 1975f).

The publication of the July 9 plan triggered in a few days the end of the Vasco Gonçalves coalition government. In a domino reaction, it led to the paralysis of the Supreme Revolutionary Council and to the fading away for the time being of the MFA General Assembly that had adopted "the people's power plan." The PCP defined the constitution elaborated by the First Engineers Regiment as "a creative intervention," and the PRP-BR, Carvalho's favorite left-wing radical group, rejoiced in seeing the political parties put into their proper place. The PDP defined the project as antidemocratic inasmuch as the "arm-raising open vote" would only give activist minorities the chance to terrorize majorities; and the PS saw it as an expression of contempt for the real people's power, which had been expressed in the April 25, 1975, general elections. The socialists suspended their participation in the government having neither obtained satisfaction in the *República* affair nor accepted the July 9 project, which violated the agreement between the MFA and the political parties. Their slogan *"É Preciso Respeitar a Vontade Popular"* ("The people's will must be respected") struck a responsive reaction in the whole country.

Meanwhile, a protest movement against "the new tyranny," taking violent anticommunist forms, began to mount in the little towns and villages. The PPD, after Gonçalves' refusal to guarantee the future of the democratic institutions, left the government as well. This party was then led by a man who could not be attacked by the PCP-MDP for his "collaborationist past" as Sá Carneiro had been: Emídio Guerreiro's personal history included participation in the Spanish Civil War on the Republican side and an anti-Nazi past as a member of the French Resistance during World War II.

With only the PCP, the MDP, and two ministers hovering between the MDP and the MES left in the government, Vasco Gonçalves resigned. Thereupon the PS started to organize huge meetings in the whole country. On July 15, for the first time since the overthrow of the Caetano regime, crowds shouted their disapproval of MFA rule with such slogans as "The people is no more with the MFA!" and "Soldiers, back to the barracks!" At Braga on July 17, Soares proclaimed that Portugal must not be left at the disposal of those who wanted to transform it into a concentration camp. The PCP reacted on the spot: misjudging its own forces, the Communist Party announced that the next socialist meeting scheduled for Oporto would not be allowed to convene. On Friday July 18, the PCP-MDP mobilized all their forces to prevent the socialists from organizing their meeting. All Portugal understood that this would be a test case. Inflammatory leaflets were distributed by the communists:

> We must stop the march of the reaction on Oporto, *come what may*. . . . The socialist meeting is only a pretext for the invasion of Oporto by false socialists, murderers . . . former Salazarists, former PIDE agents.

The PCP ordered its members to block the roads leading into the city. The moment of truth had come, but it quickly passed. The socialist meeting in Oporto was a huge success.

Having lost face in Oporto, Cunhal addressed himself personally to the Communist Youth Organization, to all the party members and friends: this time the socialists must not be allowed to hold their meeting scheduled to take place on Saturday July 19, in Lisbon. A new PCP leaflet was distributed: "The Reactionary March on Lisbon Will Not Go Through!" The communists clearly banked on their strength in the capital and on the hope that the COPCON would come to their assistance. As in the case of Oporto, however, the COPCON authorized the socialist rally. The PCP-MDP members manned roadblocks closing the 27 approaches to the capital. But COPCON, jealous of their authority, took over the roadblocks and permitted the socialists to pass. Soares, triumphant— perhaps prematurely so—asked in his speech for "a unity government with the Armed Forces." He repeated that the socialist party would not enter the government with Gonçalves as prime minister. It is quite possible that the unexpected collapse of the PCP's prestige would have rendered Gonçalves' exercise of power impossible. But the demand by a civilian for the dismissal of a fellow officer awoke the spirit of MFA officers, even those who considered Gonçalves an utter failure. Some moderate MFA officers from the top institutions—the SRC and MFA General Assembly—rallied around the discredited Gonçalves.

The man considered as a likely successor to Gonçalves was Foreign Minister Melo Antunes. An intellectual nationalist major, Antunes had developed the single coherent economical project of the new regime: to provide for a slow and tightly controlled social evolution, intended to avoid evasion of capital and a stoppage of internal and foreign investments. Antunes was backed by five other members of the SRC; they also had in common a decisive antipathy for Gonçalves' politics and the feeling that the 240 men MFA General Assembly had lost touch with the country. The "Antunists" enjoyed the confidence of both President Costa Gomes and Dr. Mario Soares; seeing that Gonçalves would stay on, they resigned from the SRC.

The following meeting of the MFA General Assembly, on July 25 and 26, was unable to arrive at any decision. The military, ruling a country that longed to return to civilian rule, felt completely isolated from the nation. The utopian plans of the MFA General Assembly members and their hollow revolutionary speeches had the unreal character of a social experiment carried out in an airtight compartment. The PCP propaganda services had given them badges bearing Vasco Gonçalves' name and the slogan "Vasco, take courage!" Yet the leader's name failed to inspire a way out from the maze. The only ad hoc solution, arrived at after 18 hours of oratory, was the establishment of a triumvirate, formed by President Costa Gomes, a nationalist, Vasco Gonçalves, a communist, and Otelo de Carvalho, COPCON's radical revolutionary.

The triumvirate was given full legislative and executive powers. This was good news for President Costa Gomes, who could free himself from the irresponsible rule of a PCP-utopian-fringe-dominated MFA General Assembly. On the other hand, the two triumvirs, Gonçalves and Carvalho, neutralized each other: Gonçalves desired to stay on in power in order to achieve that peculiar type of a "people's democracy" that was the aim of his friend and mentor, the PCP Secretary General Cunhal. Carvalho dreamed of being the key figure in implementing the foggy project of a Portugal dominated by "popular assemblies," a plan of so-called direct democracy first outlined by some extreme left-wing groups, such as the PRP-BR (Antunes, 1975). For the Communist Party, the greatest danger was not Carvalho and his followers, violent idealists split among themselves and unable to agree on a coherent political blueprint. Gonçalves could deal with them: some 900 active members of the Maoist MRPP had been arrested during the summer, and other groups on the leftist fringe were temporarily banned (Expresso, 1975d). The communist leadership feared an alliance between the president and the staffs of the army, the navy, and the air force, the MFA officers gathered around Major Melo Antunes, and the Socialist Party because such a political combination could prove immensely popular and eventually force the PCP into a democratic frame of the Western type. Therefore the full impact of all the means of communication getting their clue from Cunhal's friends was immediately felt by the partisans of a democratic solution.

Already on July 28 the daily *Diário de Notícias* attacked President Costa Gomes for having declared that the MFA looked like a vanguard that had lost the bulk of its troops on the way—a warning against unrealistic extremism, clad in a military metaphor. The other important morning paper, *O Século,* equally under Cunhalist control, and four of the six Lisbon evening papers, concentrated on the same subject: that "some circles" were betraying the revolution in order to bring back two forms of fascism, and that Soares was the harbinger of this restoration; the same theme was exploited ad nauseam by the radio and TV networks, staffed by Cunhalists and Gonçalvists (that is, Cunhalists in uniform).

But the control of the press and the radio for once proved to be insufficient. Precisely at the moment when the PCP-MDP control of the means of communication attained its highest level of efficiency—July 1975—their control of the country started to crumble. It began with "insignificant" incidents in small provincial towns such as Aveiro and Rio Maior; peasants opposed the attempt of Cunhalists to seize the control of their union. Papers criticizing the peasants as "fascist-led" were burned in some villages. Communist clubs were destroyed "by the majority of the population" (Jornal Novo, 1975b); the attacks against PCP and MDP headquarters and clubs in the northern two-thirds of the country spread like wildfire: at Fafe, Cantanhede, Bombarral, Vila Nova de Famalicoa,

Povoa de Lanhoso, Santa Tirso, and elsewhere the PCP-MDP buildings were burned. Some attackers were shot by the besieged vigilantes, but on the whole there was relatively little bloodshed.

In a month some 50 PCP-MDP buildings went up in flames, and both parties disappeared as organized forces in the major part of the northern and central districts of the country and in the Azores and Medeira. For the communist press there was not the shade of a doubt that the attacks were the result of a plot concocted by "reactionary circles," the popular masses nurturing only friendly feelings for the CPC leadership (Avante!, 1975b). But the fury and the rage manifested by broad segments of the peasants and small-town artisans could not be explained by a "CIA conspiracy" or by ideological anticommunism. It was the result of the 14-month rule of PCP and MDP local worthies in small towns and villages, where the inhabitants, "maddened by bureaucratic vexations and niggling controls," simply lost patience once an example had been set of how to resist the new rulers (Daniel, 1975). A certain measure of organization could be observed only during the last phase of the anticommunist attacks.

The "peasants' revolt" was accompanied by another series of setbacks suffered by the PCP-MDP in the trade unions, a bitterly resented failure in a party pretending to speak in the name of the working class. The trade union national convention, organized in Lisbon between July 25 and 27 by the PCP-dominated Intersindical, got out of the hands of its organizers: in more than 200 local trade unions, the PCP-sponsored candidates were defeated during the elections preceding the convention. The PCP lost its grip also in the professional organizations of private firms' employees, bank clerks, pharmacists; and—worst of all—it lost its paramount influence in the National Association of Journalists. In military circles these developments were closely followed. They resulted in a public protest against the exaggerated influence still yielded by Cunhalist officers posturing as the main PCP military stronghold, the so-called "Fifth Division" of the General Staff. Led since the beginning of the summer by an enthusiastic PCP fellow-traveller, Navy lieutenant commander Ramiro Correia, the 5th division, originally charged with public relations, grew rapidly into a Cunhalist empire; it edited the MFA bulletin, faithfully following the party line. It sent all over the country "dynamization teams" (indoctrination groups) and was also responsible for an "Institute of Military Sociology" in which only orthodox Cunhalist views were studied and propagated. During July and August, the 5th division mobilized its forces in favor of a regime directed by Gonçalves-Cunhal, attacking (by implication) the president of the Republic and (openly) the Socialist Party.

These nonmilitary activities of a General Staff department convinced many undecided MFA officers that the 5th division had become a major nuisance, and its "reorganization" became one of the claims of those favoring a "pluralist socialism" and opposing the totalitarian model. Sensing the growing disaffection with the military and political pillars of the Gonçalves government-in-formation (the 5th provisory government took nearly a month to form), the heads of the Catholic hierarchy stepped up their struggle against the occupation of the episcopal broadcasting station, *Rádio Renascença*. Gonçalves could have disarmed these formidable opponents by helping the legal owners to get back their radio station, occupied by left-wing technicians. But he did not do so and thus provoked an anticommunist "crusade" headed by bishops and canons from Aveiro, Viseu, Coimbra, and, above all, Braga. The huge anti-Gonçalves processions led by churchmen all over the northern half of the country estranged the population further from the extremist prime minister still in search of a government. Vanquished by their political rivals, the Cunhalist-Gonçalvist factions were losing all credibility.

IX. TOWARD MAJORITY RULE

Finally, on August 7, Vasco Gonçalves presented the stillborn fifth provisional government. The mediocrity of its members, faceless bureaucrats, astonished the Portuguese. The Foreign Minister, Dr. Mario Ruivo, a specialist in oceanography, had been active at the FAO, the UN Organization for Food and Agriculture, but lacked diplomatic experience. Another star on this ill-fated Cabinet was an old Coimbra professor, Texeira Ribeiro, a former theoretician of Salazar corporatism—a choice that evoked socialist comments to the effect that "red Salazarism" looked not very different from the original black one. Among the national political figures, only Álvaro Cunhal, the PCP Secretary General, declared himself satisfied with the new government. It was at this time, during the first week of August, that the former foreign minister, Major Melo Antunes, and eight of his political friends among the historical MFA military leaders published their own analysis of the situation. Called "For a Nonaligned Socialism," the Antunes document gave fresh hope to the MFA staff, disgusted and frightened by the Gonçalves-Cunhal alliance but unable to imagine another progressive solution. The "document" maintained that the nationalization wave had resulted in great and growing dismay because there were not enough qualified personnel to efficiently run the new state enterprises. The violent speeding up of the revolutionary process was rending asunder the texture of social and cultural life. The revolution, in consequence, found itself in danger of losing the support of broad sectors of the population, including the intellectuals.

The Antunes document asked for an end to the "savage and anarchist forms" in which political power had been employed. It demanded respect for the result of the April 1975 general elections and warned that the politics of the Gonçalves government deepened the yawning gap between a tiny group backing Gonçalves and Cunhal and the rest of the country. The "document" also alluded to the Angolan issue, which was turning into a Portuguese problem through the flood of refugees. President Costa Gomes did not conceal his agreement with this analysis as did the Socialist Party (Jornal Novo, 1975a; Expresso, 1975c). But under the pressure of Gonçalves and Carvalho, generally at loggerheads but united this time against the "social-democratic danger," the Revolutionary Council expelled those who had signed the Antunes document.

It was an empty victory. Carvalho, feeling that the Antunes document had stolen the show and wanting to establish himself as an ideologial leader, presented on August 13 a program prepared by a few COPCON officers. This document, called "Left Alternative," bore the hallmark of PRP-BR and MES. It criticized the Antunes document for its democratic and Western orientation, and criticized the Gonçalves-Cunhal alliance for trying to establish a bureaucratic and rigidly state-controlled society. The COPCON document advocated a direct link between the "people" and the MFA through grass-roots committees and a "popular assembly" that would take the place of the legally elected Constituent Assembly. The solution to Portugal's economic ills could be found, according to the COPCON document, by the development of commercial relations with the Third World and Eastern Europe.

The publication of Carvalho's program increased the general confusion. Carvalho wanted to appear as the "people's general," opposed to the highbrow plans of Antunes, but desired to remain in saddle in case Antunes and his friends were to prevail in the struggle for power. He agreed with the suggestion of arranging meetings between officers at the São Sebastião barracks with the goal of finding a "synthesis" between the two contradictory documents, one inspired by the European socialist tradition and the other by Third World totalitarianism. Carvalho's vacillating position made him lose his popularity with the extreme left-wingers, without increasing his prestige in socialist and pro-Antunes circles. Within three weeks the future strongman of Portugal became a mere "had-been."

The Gonçalves-headed fifth provisional government soon proved itself utterly incapable of solving any of the problems facing it. During his last stay in office Gonçalves, who at his investiture ceremony had spoken about the need for "more severe acts of repression," tried to introduce a new and much stricter system of political censorship. Above all, the Gonçalvists and Cunhalists tried to prevent any open debate on the Antunes document. However, the propaganda apparatus of the PCP and the 5th division could not prevent soldiers and officers from debating the ideas set forth in the program. As the approval expressed in votes at most of the military units gathered momentum, the days of the Gonçalves government were numbered. As the hope of using Gonçalves for the seizure of power had gone, the PCP leadership looked for an alternative strategy. The new task was to "foil the attempt of the right to regain power"; or to put it less obscurely, to prevent any non-PCP-dominated government from restoring the normal conditions needed to gradually establish a form of democratic nonaligned socialism. The PCP suddenly dropped the devastating criticism of the extreme-left fringe, which only a few days previously had been described as "objectively" helping the fascists. On August 20, Cunhal stated that a new line was in the offing. Five days later the FUR, "United Revolutionary Front," was created: former enemies—orthodox communists, Trotskyites, anarchists, "spontaneists," and revolutionary populists of the PRP-BR brand—merged. The intention was, above all, to fight by all possible means the next government, which, it was assumed, would reflect in its composition the results of the April 1975 elections (Time, 1975a). The FUR had the capacity to mobilize for street demonstrations in Lisbon at least 30,000 students, young workers, and unemployed, to which the disgruntled Gonçalvists could add some 6,000-7,000 soldiers, sailors, or deserters; the PCP would still count on some thousands of workers in Lisbon and of agricultural workers from Alentejo, who could be brought into the capital at a few hours notice. Outside the Lisbon-Alentejo regions the FUR was insignificant. But in the PCP tactic calculations the capital was the "weakest link" in Portuguese politics. The communists' great hope was to win over from a politically discredited Carvalho the elite COPCON regiments that guarded the approaches to Lisbon. Junior Gonçalvist officers had, in the meantime, distributed to left-wing vigilantes some 30,000 automatic weapons stolen from army stores "for the good of the revolution."

Having desperately tried to make his government popular by a string of demagogic measures—reduction of the price of agricultural fertilizers, rise in the salaries of minor state officials, abolition of some high school examinations—he was finally prevailed upon to resign, but only after President Costa Gomes had promised to nominate him chief of the general staff. A few days later, it had become apparent that the army would not have him. At long last Vasco Gonçalves must have realized that a country belonging to Western Europe could not be transformed into a people's democracy in the absence of a foreign occupation force (Fabião, 1975).

The activities of the 5th division were also brought to an end: on August 27 its premises were taken over by a COPCON unit, the RIOQ (Queluz Operational Infantry Regiment). It was explained that the measure had been taken pending a reorganization of the military public relations center. Meanwhile, FUR had noisily expelled the communist party from its midst for reasons of "revolutionary tactics"; but the PCP front-organization, the MDP, stayed inside the FUR acting as a link between the communists and the main factions of the extreme left. Their activity during the governmental interregnum was directed mainly toward the army, the goal being to win over the junior offices to the idea of a new revolutionary coup.

A sign of success was the refusal of many military police units to let soldiers be flown to Angola, as ordered by the Revolutionary Council, in order to save the Portuguese civilians trapped in the civil war. The most important achievement of the FUR was the appearance in September 1975 of a revolutionary soldiers' organization, the SUV (United Soldiers Will Vanquish). Directed by the unofficial PCP-extreme-left alliance, the SUV tried to foil the attempts by loyalist army units to fulfill the orders of the legal authorities. On September 6, President Costa Gomes, with the aim of strengthening the central military institution, had reshuffled the Revolutionary Council, which was from then on composed by seven Gonçalvists, seven officers leaning toward the Antunes project, and six nonpolitical technicians. It was hoped that the formation of the sixth provisional government, headed by Admiral Pinheiro de Azevedo, would make it easier to pass from revolutionary hysteria and utopianism to rational politics. The new prime minister, a 58-year-old Angola-born sailor, concealed behind the façade of a blunt sea-wolf a subtle common sense not unlike that of his good friend, President Costa Gomes. The Azevedo government numbered 14 ministers: four were MFA men: Melo Antunes (Foreign Affairs) Almeida e Costa (Interior Administration), Tomás Rosa (Labor) and Vítor Alves (without portfolio); four belonged to the Socialist Party: Dr. Jorge Campinos (Foreign Trade), Lopes Cardoso (Agriculture and Fisheries), Dr. Salgado Zenha (Finance), and Walter Rosa (Transportation and Communication); three nonaffiliated ministers followed: Marques do Carmo, an old anti-Salazarist (Industry); Dr. Almeida Santos (Social Communication, that is, Information), and Dr. Pinheiro Farinha (Justice); the two social-democrats were PPD leaders Magalhães Mota (Internal Commerce) and Dr. Sá Borges (Social Affairs); the lone communist minister was Veiga de Oliveira (Expresso, 1975b).

It became immediately clear that the PCP, though represented in the government, would oppose it whenever it liked, since the "bourgeois" rule of representative democracy and ministerial responsibility were not binding a genuine revolutionary party. The extreme left did not in any case recognize the legality of a government expressing the will of the majority ("petty-bourgeois electoralism"). As the fiery leader of the PRP-BR, Isabel do Carmo, made it clear in late October 1975: "there must be an armed insurrection" (Time, 1975a).

The Portuguese government reacted to the attempt to turn COPCON into an ally of the movement against military discipline by creating a new command intervention force, the AMI *(Agrupamento Militar de Intervenção),* which was less radical than the old COPCON. COPCON had been destroyed by the FUR, the SUV, and other PCP-extreme left "groups of dynamization" with their dreams of an immediate socialist revolution that would turn impoverished Portugal overnight into a land of plenty, justice, righteousness, and fantasy, such as described in Thomas More's *Utopia.*

Portugal, one of the oldest states in the world, is heir to a long and unbroken West European tradition. The last general elections of April 1975, which proved the political maturity of the nation, only confirm this. No lasting solution will be found to the crisis without reverting to constitutional practices. The claim to rule by virtue of superior force only invites a succession of military coups. After 48 years of Salazar-Caetano rule, Portugal has a strong aversion to any kind of tyranny. The Portuguese know that they can achieve a higher standard of living, a more open society, a real democratic control of army and government, and a more equitable distribution of wealth only if there is not a new dictatorship.

NOTES

1. The best books on the socioeconomic history of Portugal in the preindustrial era are Boxer (1969), Godinho (1964; 1963-1965), Mauro (1960), and Silbert (1967).

2. Two modern basic works on Portugal's political history are Marques (1972) and Payne (1973).

3. The best study of the 1910 revolution is Wheeler (1972).

4. The first Portuguese republic receives a fair and balanced judgment in Marques (undated).

5. Kay (1960) is a somewhat uncritical study; Fryer and Pinheiro (1961) is less flattering.

6. The official exponent of this view under Salazar was Nogueira. His book (1967) is preceded by an introduction by Dean Acheson. For a devastating criticism of present-day theories about Portugal's "Third-World character" see Lourenço (1975).

7. The best bibliographical work on revolutionary ideologies in the colonial empire is Chilcote (1969).

8. With respect to the organic weakness of Portugal's economic structure and its social fallout, see Castro (1974), Rocha (1965), and Cunhal (1968).

9. A bibliography of works, leaflets, and illegal papers published by the illegal anti-Salazarist resistance does not yet exist; with respect to victims of Salazarist repression see Rodrigues (1974), Soares (1972) [the socialist view], and Carvalhas et al. (1974) [a Catholic view].

10. The structures of the Salazarist regime are lovingly described by one of their architects (Caetano, 1972); a more objective study is Woolf (1969: 302-336).

11. The best explanation of the principles directing this type of regime is given by the director himself (Salazar, 1944-1967).

12. For the official view of the army before the start of the colonial wars of the sixties, see Figueiredo (1961). A test case is given by Marques (1975). Regarding the mentality of the future authors of the April coup see Banazol (1974).

13. An apologia for the PIDE is found in Caetano (1974: 76-80). A description of its functioning by its victims is in Rodrigues (1974). Expresso published interesting material about the PIDE in its issues after the April 1974 coup.

14. Sketchy information about the students' political activity in opposition to Salazar is found in Carvalhas et al. (1974). On universities, see Marques (1972: II, 142-144, 204-206).

15. Banazol (1974) is a lieutenant-colonel who wrote his recollections before a more official and revolutionary version of the origins of the coup gained in importance. His little book is fresh, unpretentious, and instructive.

16. On the PIDE's role in Cabral's assassination see Crimi (1975: 18-21). This article, published five weeks before Spinola's alleged putsch, charges two of the general's close supporters, Firmino Miguel and Almeida Bruno, with coresponsibility for the murder. On Otelo de Carvalho's admiration for the shooting of reactionaries by Cabral's heirs, see The Times (1975a).

17. The Ultramar Combatants and the Portuguese Legion considered Caetano's government not tough enough in dealing with the African rebellions or with internal opposition (Caetano, 1974: 68-69).

18. Semprun (1975) states that on the eve of the April coup Caetano had been abandoned even by the strata of the bourgeoisie most faithful to the Estado Novo.

19. Caetano, too, believed in such a future "Commonwealth," but was afraid to say so (see Baptista, 1973). In his last TV speech, March 28, 1974, the prime minister hinted at a future evolution of the Ultramar "in accordance with the progress made and with world conditions."

20. Carvalho, still a captain the day after the coup he helped to organize, pretended that Spínola "had been informed about nothing." But without Spínola's consent the success of the coup would have been far more problematic. See Semprun (1975: 27).

21. Before the Spínola intentona, the Caldas da Rainha intentona (failed coup) was hailed as the "1905" of the April "1917"; after Spínola's failure, the Caldas da Rainha affair was seen as an a priori Spínolist failure, even by Carvalho himself; see Expresso (1975i).

22. In February 1975, the Caldas da Rainha episode was already considered not sufficiently important to be mentioned in an official list of actions and risings against the old regime (Ministry of Mass Communication, 1975).

23. Ruas (1974) has the best hour-by-hour account of the coup. For a more serene summing-up, see Publicaçõe Europa-América (1975).

24. The members of the junta were known as traditional Portuguese officers, which explains the protests of the anticolonialist movements against the new regime, whose revolutionary nature they did not know (Keesing's Contemporary Archives, 1974: 26519).

25. See Le Monde (1974b) and other prominent European papers on April 26. The links between a part of the MFA officers and the PCP were not stressed by the press.

26. It appears that the MFA officers who knew early on that it would be impossible to collaborate with Spínola were Melo Antunes and Rosa Coutinho (Expresso, 1975i).

27. Gonçalves is the son of a foreign exchange banker, and his background is "distinctly middle class"; but first of all he is a member of the officer corps and more than probably a PCP member, rather on the dogmatic side (see Time, 1975b; Corriere della Sera, 1975a; Le Monde, 1975a).

28. For information on Portugal, the brilliant Yale professor of sociology Juan Linz and his disciples have stated throughout the last 15 years that Salazarist Portugal would reform from within (Maxwell, 1975a).

29. The paradox of the situation was that Malawi had been the only black-ruled country where Portugal had had an embassy, thanks to Jardim.

30. According to the Times (1974a), there were some 60 killed and 427 injured during the riots in Mozambique. On September 9 The Times (1974b) wrote in a leading article that "the rising is irresponsible . . . their [the rebels'] most likely ambition is to detach the southern area of the country [and] to form it into a white-ruled . . . possibly client state of South Africa."

31. At another place in the same book, Caetano (1974: 93) complains that his own regime protected the bourgeoisie so well that it lost all its *"espírito combativo."*

32. An attempt to convince world public opinion that Portuguese colonialism serves the cause of human progress is found in Nogueira (1963).

33. The foreign press noticed with interest that Sr. Cunhal expected and almost prophesied the coming coup (Le Monde, 1975b, 1975c).

34. The best on-the-spot description of the March 11 affair in the international press seems to be the reports of Bernardo Valli (1975), Lisbon correspondent of the Corriere della Sera, published by his paper in three parts beginning with the March 12 issue.

35. The Lisbon correspondent of the French weekly writes that Spínola, before departing for Spain, affirmed that "they had deceived him." Captain Salgueiro Maia, one of the heroes of the April 1974 coup, defines the March 11 intentona as "a mystery." Backmann (1975) describes the failed putsch as "astonishing," Spínola as "betrayed," and the whole affair as a chance for the MFA to assume full control. The Times (1975b) wrote that "the army's attitude has drawn suspicion on itself," and adds that the coup had suddenly given the green light to those wanting immediate, full nationalization.

36. Oliveira had asked for a radical purge already after the resignation of Spínola (Expresso, 1974c).

37. A Capital, a Lisbon daily, knew about the MFA officers' intention to impose such a

"platform of agreement" on the political parties already on February 7, two months before the signing of the formal document and, of course, before Spínola's intentona (which was used by the MFA to justify an "agreement," to which only one side really agreed). See Newsweek (1974). The establishment of the Supreme Revolutionary Council was decided in order to completely militarize the highest institution of the state.

38. Already during the first hours after Spínola's failure, the Portuguese authorities knew perfectly well that "the capitalists" stood behind the general (Tiempo [Mexico], 1975). Ambassador Carlucci called the attack on Spínola "a well-oiled, well-directed smear campaign" (Time, 1975b).

39. The French press and specially Le Monde, generally sympathetic to Third World and anti-NATO causes, became the favorite organ of MFA spokesmen in order to diffuse their views abroad. The British and American press were considered to be biased against dictatorships, and the Italian press to be detrimentally influenced by Berlinguer's conception of communism.

REFERENCES

ANTUNES, C. (1975) "Frente e' plataforma táctica," Jornal Novo (August 28).
Avante! (1974) "Firmes nos princípios, unidos na acção, confiantes no futuro," (October 21).
——— (1975a) "Um livro indispensável!" (October 21).
——— (1975b) Article (July 26).
BACKMANN, R. (1975) "Du bon usage d'un complot," Le Nouvel Observateur (March 17).
BANAZOL, L.A. (1974) A Origem do Movimento das Forças Armadas. Lisbon: Prelo.
BAPTISTA, A.A. (1973) Conversas com Marcelo Caetano. Lisbon: Livraria Morais Editora.
BAPTISTA, J. (1975) Caminhos para uma revolução. Lisbon: Livraria Bertrand.
BIANCHI, L. (1975a) "Berlinguer: non siamo d'accordo." Corriere della Sera (July 13).
——— (1975b) "Tutti gli occhi sul Portogallo." Corriere della Sera (May 21).
BOXER, C.R. (1969) The Portuguese Seaborne Empire: 1415-1825. New York: Knopf.
CABRAL, A. (1973) Return to the Source: Selected Speeches by Amilcar Cabral. New York: Monthy Review Press.
——— (1972) Our People Are Our Mountains. London: Com. for Freedom.
——— (1971) Rapport bref sur la situation de la lutte. Conakry: Partido Africano de Indepência.
CAETANO, M. (1974) Depoimento. Rio de Janeiro. Distribuidora Record.
——— (1972) Manual de Ciência Política (6th ed.), 2 vol. Lisbon: Coimbra Editora.
CAL, M. de la (1975) "The fall of the 20 families." Time (July 14).
CARVALHAS, C et al. (1974) 48 Anos de Fascismo em Portugal. Lisbon: Livraria Ler.
CASTRO, A. (1974) Sobre o capitalismo português (2nd ed.). Coimbra: Atlantida.
CHILCOTE, R.H. (1969) Emerging Nationalism in Portuguese Africa. Stanford: Hoover Inst. Press.
Corriere della Sera (1975a) Article (July 28).
——— (1975b) Article (July 27).
——— (1975c) "Tutti gli occhi sul Portogallo." (May 21).
CRIMI, B. (1975) "Deux ans après—la verité sur l'assassinat d'Amilcar Cabral." Jeune Afrique (January 31).
CUNHAL, A. (1975) Discursos Políticos (vol II). Lisbon: Ediçoês AVANTE!
——— (1974a) Radicalismo Pequeno Burgues de Fachada Socialista—Documentos Políticos do Partido Comunista Português. Lisbon: Ediçoês AVANTE!

88

——— (1974b) Rumo à Vitória. Lisbon: A Opinia.

——— (1968) A Questo Agrária em Portugal. Rio de Janeiro: Civilização Brasileira.

Daily Telegraph (1974) "Portugal breaks with Malawi." (July 24).

DANIEL, J. (1975) "L'armée Portugaise face à l'anti-communisme." Le Nouvel Observateur (August 11).

DAVIDSON, B. (1973) In the Eye of the Storm: Angola's People. New York: Doubleday.

Der Spiegel (1974a) "Die armée will keine rache." (No. 44).

——— (1974b) Article (No. 23).

Diário de Lisboa (1974a) Article (July 12).

——— (1974b) Articles (May 22).

——— (1974c) Articles (May 21).

Diário de Noticias (1974a) Articles (June 10).

——— (1974b) Articles (June 9).

——— (1974c) Articles (June 8).

DOMINGUES, F.B. (1975) "Católico e Socialista." Portugal Socialista (April 20).

ERMAKOV, V. (1975) "Portugalskya Gorizonty." Pravda (May 25).

Expresso (1975a) Article (December 21).

——— (1975b) "VI Governo provisório toma (finalmente) posse." (September 20).

——— (1975c) "Amplo apoio ao documento dos 9." (August 9).

——— (1975d) "E agora, Mário Soares?" (July 26).

——— (1975e) "Fernand Oneto fala ao Expresso sobre o caso da Comissão de Extinção e dos arquivos da Pide." (July 12).

——— (1975f) "A expêriencia piloto da zona do RE 1." (July 12).

——— (1975g) "Rosa Coutinho ao Congresso da Indústria." (July 12).

——— (1975h) "Entrevista com Aquino de Bragança." (May 10).

——— (1975i) "Movimento das forças armadas–das ambiguidades do programa a definição socialista." (April 25).

——— (1975j) "Um ano depois a esperança mantém-se." (April 25).

——— (1975k) "Nomeados 18 membros do Conselho de Imprensa." (April 25).

——— (1975l) "Do valor do voto em branco à constituição de um exercito popular." (April 25).

——— (1975m) "Galvão de Melo: franco-atirador, cavaleiro e pianista." (April 19).

——— (1975n) "Campanha eleitoral em doze frentes." (April 19).

——— (1975o) "Nacionalizar não chega; é necessário que os trabalhadores controlem." (April 19).

Expresso (1974a) "Expresso descreve a estruturn e função do MFA." (December 21).

——— (1974b) "Do socialismo em liberdade a revolução socialista." (December 21).

——— (1974c) October 26.

——— (1974d) "A longa noite de 27-28 de Setembro–nos bastidores da historia." (October 5).

——— (1974e) "A conspiraçao do fim-de-semana." (September 28).

——— (1974f) "As primeras relações de pessoas detidas." (September 28).

——— (1974g) "MAP preparava um atentado contra o primeiro-ministro." (September 28).

FABIÃO, C. (1975) Article in A Capital (September 2).

FALLACI, O. (1975) Article in Time (July 28).

FERREIRA, M. (1975) "Não é por se transformar em cooperativa que uma empresa doente se cura." Expresso (July 5).

FIGUEIREDO, M.H. de (1961) The Portuguese Armed Forces Lisbon: Min. da Defesa Nacional.

FRYER, P. and P.M. PINHEIRO (1961) Oldest Ally: A Portrait of Salazar's Portugal. London: D. Dobson.

89

GODINHO, M. (1963-1965) Os descobrimentos e a economia mudial (2 vols.). Lisbon: Arcadia.

— — (1964) L'Economie de l'Empire Portugais Paria: S.E.V.P.E.N.

HAMMOND, R.J. (1966) Portugal and Africa (1815-1910), A Study in Uneconomic Imperialism. Stanford: Stanford Univ. Press.

HOOK, S. (1975) "What the cold war was about." Encounter (March).

Jornal Novo (1975a) Article (August 8).

— — (1975b) "Avéiro e Rio Maior são notícia." (July 19).

KAY, H. (1970) Salazar and Modern Portugal. London: Eyre & Spottiswoode.

Keesing's Contemporary Archives (1974).

Le Monde (1975a) July 30.

— — (1975b) March 14.

— — (1975c) March 13.

— — (1974a) October 3.

— — (1974b) April 27.

— — (1974c) April 23.

— — (1974d) April 16.

— — (1974e) April 12.

— — (1974f) March 18.

Le Nouvel Observateur (1975a) Interview with Santiago Carrillo (June 23).

— — (1975b) "Le Portugal vu par un communiste italien." (June 2).

LOURENCO, E. (1975) "Socialismo critico ou ditadura: a margem de um Portugal nu." (May 3).

MARQUES, A.H. (1975) General Sousa Dias. Lisbon: D. Quixote.

— — (1973) Historia de Portugal (2 vols.). [The Portuguese work is slightly different from the American edition that preceded it.] Lisbon: Vol. I Edicoes Agora. Vol. II Palas Editores.

— — (1972) History of Portugal (2 vols.) New York: Columbia Univ. Press.

— — (undated) A Primeira República Portuguesa—para uma visao estrutural. Lisbon: Livros Horizonte.

MARTINET, G. (1975) "Populisme militaire et socialisme démocratique." Le Nouvel Observateur (July 28).

MAURO, F. (1960) Le Portugal et l'Atlantique au XVII siecle (1570-1670). Paris: S.E.V.P.E.N.

MAXWELL, K. (1975a) "Portugal under pressure." New York Review of Books (May).

— — (1975b) "The hidden revolution in Portugal." New York Review of Books (April 17).

Ministry of Mass Communication (1975) Portugal, Freedom Year One: Lisbon.

NEWITT, M.D.D. (1973) Portuguese Settlement on the Zambesi. New York: Holmes & Meyer.

Newsweek (1975) April 14.

New York Times (1974) September 13.

NOGUEIRA, A.F. (1967) The Third World. London: Johnson.

— — (1963) The United Nations and Portugal: A Study of Anti-Colonialism. London: Sidgwick & Jackson.

OECD Economic Survey (1974) July.

O Seculo (1974a) December 14.

— — (1974b) October 19.

— — (1974c) September 27.

— — (1974d) August 21.

90

PAYNE, S.G. (1973) A History of Spain and Portugal (2 vols.). Madison, Wisconsin: Univ. of Wisconsin Press.

PINTADO, X. (1964) The Structure and Growth of the Portuguese Economy. Geneva.

Portugal Socialista (1975a) May 1.

——— (1975b) April 23.

Publicacões Europa-América (1975) Livro do Ano 1974—factos e homens protagonistas de un ano. Lisbon.

República (1974) September 11.

ROCHA, N. (1965) Franca: A Emigração Dolorosa. Lisbon: Ulisseia.

RODRIGUES, A., et al. (1975) O Movimento dos Capitres e o 25 de Abril. Lisbon: Moraes.

RODRIGUES, M.F. (1974) Tarrafal Aldeia da Morte. Oporto: Brasilia Editora.

RUAS, H.B. [ed.] (1975) A Revolução das Flores. Lisbon: Aster.

SALAZAR, A. (1944-1967) Discursos (6 vols.). Coimbra: Coimbra Editora.

SANTOS, I.T.E. and M.T. BAGULHO (1975) "Pouca gente para mudar os campos?" Expresso (April 25).

SEMPRUN, J. (1975) La Guerre Sociale au Portugal. Paris: Editions Champ Libre.

SILBERT, A. (1967) Le Portugal mediterraneen à la fin de l'ancien régime (2 vols.). Paris.

SILVA, H.V. de (1975) "Um ano depois: que imprensa temos?" Expresso (April 25).

SILVA, V.J. (1975) "Uma sociadade em crise de transformação busca o seu 'modelo' revolucionário." Expresso (April 25).

SOARES, M. (1972) Le Portugal Baillonne. Paris: Calmann-Levy.

SOUSA, M.R. de (1975a) "O 1 de Maio de 18% dos portugueses." Expresso (May 3).

——— (1975b) "Rosa Coutinho e o socialismo não alinhado." Expresso (April 25).

——— (1975c) "Soldados e operários reunem-se em congresso." Expresso (April 19).

SPÍNOLA, A. de (1974) Portugal e o Futuro. Lisbon: Livraria Bertrand.

Tiempo (1975) March 24.

Time (1975a) "Brigades—voices of chaos." (October 20).

——— (1975b) March 24.

The Times (1975a) June 20.

——— (1975b) March 12.

TREND, J.B. (1957) Portugal. London.

VALLI, B. (1975) Reports in Corriere della Sera (March 12, 13, 14).

WHEELER, D. (1972) "The Portuguese revolution of 1910." J. of Modern History (No. 44).

WHEELER, D. and R. PELISSIER (1971) Angola. London: Pall Mall.

WOOLF, S.J. [ed.] (1968) European Fascism. New York: Random House.